The Nature of Maps

Arthur H. Robinson and
Barbara Bartz Petchenik

The Nature of Maps

Essays toward Understanding Maps and Mapping

The University of Chicago Press

Chicago and London

ARTHUR H. ROBINSON is Lawrence Martin Professor of Cartography at the University of Wisconsin, Madison. He is president of the International Cartographic Association and past president of the Association of American Geographers. He is the author of many professional papers and books, including *The Look of Maps* and *Elements of Cartography*.

BARBARA BARTZ PETCHENIK, now on the staff of Cartographic Services, R. R. Donnelley & Sons, Chicago, received her Ph.D. from the University of Wisconsin, Madison. As cartographic editor of *World Book Encyclopedia*, she conducted research in fundamental cognitive aspects of map reading. She is cartographic editor, *Atlas of Early American History: The Revolutionary Era, 1760-1790*, and has published many articles in professional journals.

The University of Chicago Press, Chicago 60637
The University of Chicago Press, Ltd., London
© 1976 by The University of Chicago
All rights reserved. Published 1976
Printed in the United States of America
80 79 78 77 76   9 8 7 6 5 4 3 2 1

Library of Congress Cataloging in Publication Data

Robinson, Arthur Howard, 1915–
    The nature of maps.

    Bibliography: p.
    Includes index.
    1. Cartography.   2. Maps.   I. Petchenik, Barbara Bartz, joint author.   II. Title.
GA105.3.R62   526   75-36401
ISBN 0-226-72281-3

Contents

v

Preface

The range of comprehension for any individual human being is rather limited, the environment experienced directly rather small, but there have always been some individuals who have attempted to transcend the limitations of the bounded personal milieu. They have searched for ways of encoding human experience in order to produce knowledge that would facilitate more general understanding of the spatial and temporal aspects that bear upon individual and collective human existence in complex and multitudinous ways. With the passing of time, formal fields of study coalesced around particular aspects of man's interests, giving rise to the *content* of branches of knowledge such as history, geography, and the sciences. At the same time, various *forms* of symbolization developed, providing the means for expressing and communicating emotional and intellectual insights. Within the domain of symbolic form there is a considerable range of possibility, extending from the almost purely cognitive notation of mathematics, through spoken and written language, to the almost purely expressive forms of music and the graphic arts. The form of symbolization with special utility for encoding and transmitting human knowledge of the environment is mapping.

No matter what medium we use, it is important that we be able to communicate clearly and precisely, and we are more likely to do so when we are explicitly aware of the character of the medium. In writing about the importance of studying language, Adams (1974) pointed out that such study is no less practical than any other study. He observed: "The fact is that, in the conditions under which we live, and in the conditions of any materially prosperous civilization, if you want to eat, you have to be able to communicate. No tickee, no washee." This need for successful communication surely applies to mapping.

During most of the long history of cartography, cartographers have been chiefly concerned with technical problems: acquiring and

vii

perfecting geographic data, devising ways of symbolizing it, and inventing methods of mechanically preparing and duplicating the physical map. Remarkably little concern was ever expressed about how a map actually accomplished what it was supposed to do—communicate. To be sure, an occasional cartographer wondered about the effectiveness of the maps he created, and some devised new ways of presenting information cartographically because they were personally dissatisfied with the way it had been done before. A clear example of such an innovation, uncomplicated by previous convention, is Adolphe Quetelet's introduction in 1829 of continuous shading to portray the areal variations in the frequency of social phenomena in order to give what he thought would be a more effective view than Charles Dupin's first use of the choroplethic technique three years earlier. Although there are numerous similar examples of singular communicative innovations, especially during the past two hundred years, only rarely were these developed from or accompanied by carefully reasoned analyses.

Furthermore, for every one such novel idea there were thousands of maps made with little or no thought given to the images evoked in the minds of those who looked at them. Generally speaking, until recently the way in which a map accomplishes what its maker intends, and how it relates to other forms of knowing and communicating, have not been subjects for study, least of all by cartographers. In one sense, there is some justification for W. M. Davis's complaint (1924) that the inarticulateness of maps seems to have affected their makers.

This is not to say that cartographers have allowed their field to become conventionalized or stereotyped: quite the contrary. Innovation has succeeded innovation, at a rapid and increasing rate, literally revolutionizing cartography in the modern era. The field is being flooded with new ideas and techniques. Many of these are not merely better ways of doing old things; they involve totally new kinds of maps and would therefore seem to demand more astute analyses of some of the basic processes involved. For example, the orthophotomap is a fundamentally different kind of map from the conventional topographic "line" map it is superseding. For the first time in the history of cartography the map viewer looks from above at a continuous "natural" surface image—with which he is largely unfamiliar—instead of at a contrived, symbolic representation. The cognitive significance of this is probably profound, but it has not been much studied. In the area of methodology, such processes as generalization, map comparison, and cartographic design, to mention but a few, are appropriate subject matter for critical review. Nevertheless, even though there are active researchers in both applied and basic aspects of the field, serious deficiencies, which become more apparent when we turn our attention to some general objectives of research, still need study.

Research in communication can be carried out for two distinct and different purposes. The first is to gain specific understandings that will lead to improvements in practical information transmission, and to solutions of limited problems. In cartography this includes the psychophysical investigations of scaling symbols and the comparison of the communicative effectiveness of various types of maps. The second objective of research is to acquire understanding of a more general and fundamental nature that can be used to augment or construct comprehensive theory. Such research includes the study of communication by means of maps (sometimes called "metacartography"), and often seems of little or no immediate practical applicability. On the other hand, research done for the first purpose, practical application, often contributes little to the progress of theory development.

It is our firm belief that there is an urgent need for a general theory of cartography. Such a theory would provide a basic structure for the field of mapping, would give relevance and location to research done in pursuit of the first goal, and would make clear the areas that need further investigation. Our essays are intended, therefore, to be a kind of introduction to a theory of cartography. No one could be more conscious than we are of their incompleteness and deficiencies, and perhaps their brevity is a reflection of these characteristics. Nevertheless, we feel it necessary to begin this way.

The range of graphic or visual communication-representation systems is considerable, and cartography is only one small portion of it. The amount of time the average person spends looking at maps in his three-score-plus years is minute compared to the hours he spends looking at photographs or television. Yet we conclude, and argue here, that maps are fundamental in a way that no other image is. The term "mapping" is often used metaphorically in an abstract, non-cartographic sense to connote organizing, planning, presenting, and knowing. Students of verbal communication have frequently resorted to "mapping" as a fundamental analogy and as something apparently so basic that to us it seems well worth careful philosophical and psychological consideration. Perhaps our findings will have implications for other forms of graphic communication.

It is not our intention in this book to suggest what mapping should be, or what cartographers should do when making maps. Rather, we attempt to begin to make explicit what has been implicit. Mapping is based on systems of assumptions, on logic, on human needs, and on human cognitive characteristics, very little of which has been recognized or discussed in cartography. Intuition, not analysis, has dominated the cartographer's field. There is nothing at all wrong with intuition (or art, if the usual art/science dichotomy in cartography is invoked). Most of the time intuition works well, and often we not even aware of its role. But when it doesn't work, we must then resort to analysis. Analysis can supplement, enrich, and broaden intuitive activity, and the use we make of intuitive creations; but it cannot replace intuition. Analysis can sometimes be used to determine the explicit nature of a problem, but solutions most often arise from intuitive activity. Prints, paintings, and other complex images perceptible through vision are thought to be activities with strong intuitive components in their preparation as well as their perception, and perhaps because maps have been most strongly associated with such images, they too have been thought to be the results of intuitive processes. But the real reason for this belief may simply be that the cognitive character of maps has not been sufficiently studied. We think it likely that many design decisions in cartography will always be nondeducible in the direct sense, because of the overwhelming "simultaneous complexity" of the perceptual array involved. But we also believe that the development of sharp insight and intuitive judgment on the part of the individual cartographer will be greatly facilitated by an understanding of the communication process and the psychological and physiological bases underlying the perception of the map.

The need for a thorough understanding of the cognitive character of the map was not nearly so important in earlier times. Until recently most maps were relatively simple, showing the locations of some things with respect to others. As thematic cartography has developed, however, it has become necessary for us to be concerned with the depiction of highly abstract, nonvisual phenomena and relationships, and with the representation of subtle distinctions. Furthermore, the perfection of electronic scanning from satellites and the orthophotoscope has made available a whole new range of cartographic opportunity. The increasing role of computer assistance in mapping and the possibilities of automatic plotter drawings and cathode ray tube displays add an additional dimension. Yet although they enhance our capabilities enormously, machines cannot intuit and must be told what to do at every step of the way. As cartography becomes more and more complex, the analytical and intuitive effort needed to produce successsful maps will increase. We believe that to move forward significantly we must have a deeper understanding of the characteristics and processes by which the map acquires meaning from its maker and evokes meaning in its user—a general theory of cartography. We hope that we will help to move in that direction.

This project has been under way for more than five years and has required a good deal of learning on our part. Much of this has come from colleagues in cartography, both personally and through the extensive literature that, fortunately, has been growing in recent years. Our debt to the literature especially relevant to the specific subjects of the essays is only partly indicated by the list of references, since many other works from past and present students of cartography, not included in the list, have helped to mold our general ideas and convictions. Personally, we gratefully acknowledge the formal and informal contributions of Drs. Joel Morrison, Phillip Muehrcke, Judy Olson, and David Woodward. Many others, including, Henry Castner, Gerald Fremlin, Peter Van Demark, Carleton Cox, and numerous students contributed greatly by bouncing back ideas with imaginative new twists. Mary E. Robinson made many useful suggestions and performed admirably in the tedious checking and proofing of manuscript.

We are pleased also to acknowledge the material assistance without which we could not have completed or, as a matter of fact, even started the project. The Graduate School of the University of Wisconsin-Madison, through its Research Committee and the Lawrence Martin Professorship of Cartography, provided both of us generous support. Field Enterprises Educational Corporation did likewise and the Newberry Library gave precious time. An especially grateful acknowledgement goes to Mrs. June Bennett: this little book, per page, probably has set a world's record for rough drafts, photocopying, and shuttling between the authors. Her expertise and willingness may also have set a world's record.

1 On Maps and Mapping

Above all, to insist on having the meaning of a word clearly understood before using it, and the meaning of a proposition before assenting to it; these are the lessons we learn from ancient dialecticians.

John Stuart Mill

The apparent simplicity of an ordinary sketch map is deceptive; in fact, even the simplest map is a remarkably complicated instrument for understanding and communicating about the environment. It is quite reasonable to suppose that the map, as a communicative device, has been around as long as written language has: like writing, a map is a way of graphically expressing mental concepts and images. On the other hand, whereas language has had the benefit of numerous penetrating studies of its form and function, the map has not. Consequently, for something both venerable and common, the map seems to be surprisingly mysterious.

As we have pursued an analysis of the map as a basic form of communication, a curious contradiction has become apparent. Cartographers and geographers, who of all people ought to know about maps, seem least sure of the map's character—for example, an article by Zelinsky, a well-known geographer, is titled "The First and Last Frontier of Communication: The Map as Mystery"—while other students in such fields as psychology, philosophy, and semantics seem simply to take the proposition "map" for granted. In this first chapter we shall review this easy acceptance at some length in order to determine whether other fields have discovered some basic unifying concept.

We shall attempt to state here the purposeful context in which lie the other, more particular essays of this book. In order to do this, and to prepare the ground, we shall have to define some terms rather carefully, because one of the troubles with writing or talking about cartography and maps is that the ordinary terminology is not sufficiently precise for our purposes. Often the imprecise connotations of a word, such as "mapper," can be very confusing when one is trying to deal carefully with a complex subject. In addition, we shall comment on some of the specific ideas to be examined in later sections. This, then, is a kind of preparation.

The traveler into an uncharted region should carefully examine all potentially useful information about that area, in the hope that some data will be relevant to problems he may face. An ambitious excursion into the realm of cartographic concepts and theory requires a similar survey. Initially we are particularly concerned with the questions *What is a map?* and *Where does the map fit into the larger system of cognition in general?* It seemed appropriate, therefore, first to examine the philosophical literature representative of the thinking in such fields as cartography, geography, language and semantics, psychology, and the philosophy of science, to determine how others have looked at maps. From the accumulation of these ideas the curious pattern noted above emerged. While some cartographers and geographers have cast about for things to which they can liken the map, in order that they may gain additional insight into it and the cartographic process in general, scholars in other fields tend to use the map as *the* fundamental analogy.

The literature of geography and cartography is replete with statements extolling the virtue of the map, sometimes with an almost religious fervor, such as Sauer's preachment (1956, p. 289):

> Show me a geographer who does not need them constantly and want them about him, and I shall have my doubts as to whether he has made the right choice of life.... Maps break down our inhibitions, stimulate our glands, stir our imagination, loosen our tongues. The map speaks across the barriers of language; it is sometimes claimed as the language of geography.

Reviews of the way students of cartography and geography have looked at maps over the years reveal little in the way of insight into the map being something extraordinary or even the recognition of that possibility (Pietkiewicz 1965). Only in recent years has the study of the map by geographers and cartographers begun to probe beyond the physical object into its theoretical foundations. The increasing concern of geographers with cognitive maps and spatial behavior (Downs and Stea 1973a) and the analogy of maps and language (Harvey 1969, pp. 369–376) is encouraging, to say the least, but it does serve to emphasize the paucity of our previous understanding.

In a strangely general/specific explanation of the map as an example of the static class of models in science, Chorley and Haggett (1967, pp. 48–49) point out that "it is characteristic that maps should be likened to languages and scientific theories ... we some-

times think of maps as models for languages and scientific theories."
A perusal of the literature certainly bears this out, as we shall see.
This is a fortunate turn of events, but more than that, a challenging
one. What can there be about the map which is so profoundly
fundamental? Why should a representational system for space be so
basic? Further, assuming that the concept "map" provides some
sort of universally accepted, fundamental datum, what simpler
analogies or definitions can we use to clarify our understanding of
it? These are difficult questions.

In most areas of knowledge, the attempt to explain that which is
more complex proceeds by analogizing what is less familiar with
what is more familiar—that is, employing simple concepts to
illuminate those which are more complicated. Unfortunately, in
writing or thinking about mapping, this is not possible. In the first
place, we cannot explain mapping by mapping or in any kind of
mapping terms. Instead we need to use a language, composed of
discrete words which follow each other either in a rigorously
arranged temporal sequence of sounds or, when written, in a linear
sequence of marks. This puts us in a difficult situation: we are
forced to use words to clarify to ourselves what mapping is all about,
and yet the language we must use is itself a different medium and is
often taken to be the more complex of these two distinct communication systems! Psycholinguistics is not an impossible field of study,
although admittedly it is a very complicated one (cf. Slobin 1971),
whereas "psychocartographics," the study of the interaction of
cognition and mapping, must employ a "foreign language" as an
analytical tool.

It has turned out to be both astonishing and frustrating for the
introspective cartographer to sample the large literature that has
sprung up in the last few decades on the general topic of communication. Maps clearly are involved in communication, and it would
seem that much could be learned from other analyses of other types
of communication. The frustration comes with the discovery that the
universal metaphor turns out to be *map* itself! Hence, when the
map is the "atom" of investigation, how can the mapper contem-
plate his own activity? Runkel provides the best example of this:

> It follows from this view that communication cannot be fruit-
> fully conceived as a sequence in which self-contained packets of
> information are exchanged. It is not a process in which one
> person merely adds to the belongings of another by "giving"
> him information. It is rather a kind of guessing game. Each

person carries with him his cognitive field as a map of the world. He responds not to the world, but to the map. When he receives the stimulus of a communication, the meaning it has is the way it can be fitted into the map. When the communication fits readily, one's confidence in his map of the world is increased. . . . Since the effects of a communication depend on the manner in which it "meshes" with an existing cognitive map, we might entertain the notion that these efforts will take place more readily when the cognitive maps of the communicators are similar in structure. [1956, pp. 178–79]

Clearly, something very fundamental is assumed about maps and the process of mapping. When non-cartographic writers use the term "map"—as, for example, when the anthropologist Hall writes, "Laying out a map of culture is a unique way of proceeding" (1959, p. 176)—they seem to mean that it is possible to take isolated incidents, experiences, and so on, and arrange them intellectually so that there is some coherence, some total relation, instead of individual isolation. Since plotting the information they have, as one would plot geographical positions on paper, gives them the knowledge they already have *plus* the sort of automatic potential organization provided by the continuous cognitive field (cf. the surface of the paper) in which the information is plotted, mapping is considered to be the most fundamental way of converting personal knowledge to transmittable knowledge. The basic significance of maps, then, seems to lie particularly in the fact that maps are surrogates of space.

As we experience space, and construct representations of it, we know that it will be continuous. Everything is somewhere, and no matter what other characteristics objects do not share, they *always* share relative location, that is, spatiality; hence the desirability of equating knowledge with space, an intellectual space. This assures an organization and a basis for predictability, which are shared by absolutely everyone. This proposition appears to be so fundamental that apparently it is simply adopted a priori.

Students in fields concerned with language systems, signs, and meanings extend the assumption of the knowledge–space–map relationship to include an assumed isomorphism between the map and cognitive spatial territory. Perhaps the prime examples of this come from students of what is called "general semantics." Without going into detail, general semantics is the study of the relation of signs (in

this case spoken and written language) to referents and the consequences in human behavior. According to its founder, Korzybski
(1941), a great many human problems stem from the use of a
language system which can be misleading (Rapoport 1952). That is,
the form of the language may not be properly matched to "reality,"
but since language tends to be accepted as reality, people are misled
by it, function less well than they should, communicate inadequately,
and so on. Maps appear to enter into this analysis in a very
fundamental way, because the relationship between the language
system and reality is analogized as that between a map and the
territory it represents. This fundamental analogy is considered to be
a universally shared known. Korzybski states it clearly when he
writes:

> Any map or language, to be of maximum usefulness, should, in
> structure, be similar to the structure of the empirical world.
> Likewise, from the point of view of a theory of sanity, any sys-
> tem or language should, in structure, be similar to the struc-
> ture of our nervous system. [1941, p. 11]

The key word is "structure." What Korzybski finds that maps retain
of the territory is structure. He goes on to say, "Two important
characteristics of maps should be noticed. A map is *not* the territory
it represents, but, if correct, it has a *similar structure* to the territory,
which accounts for its usefulness" (1941, p. 58). Structure, unfortunately, is not further defined. Apparently it is thought to be
sufficiently obvious from the example of maps so that the term need
not, and perhaps cannot, be defined more simply. We shall find
later, in a consideration of the logical relations involved in mapping
systems, that the concept of structure is very important.

Korzybski assumed that the map–territory image was simple and
needed no analysis or explanation. In his examples, "structure"
seems to mean certain kinds of spatial relationships, particularly
topological ones. He equates language with a map because the
former is assumed to preserve certain relations which exist in an
intellectual sort of space. Further scrutiny of this whole analogy,
quite central to Korzybski's thinking, reveals that cartographically it
is so elementary as to be of questionable utility. While stressing that
the map is not *the* territory, he seems to forget that a map is *a*
territory, and that it may be meaningful to employ a variety of
transformations to retain particular relationships from one territory
to the other. Reality and language must, therefore, *both* be con-

verted into some kinds of spaces before one can be mapped on the other.

Students of general semantics frequently invoke the map–territory relation in a variety of contexts, and some of their applications help to clarify their conception of the analogy. Exton explains the difference between a word which stands for something in the case where there is no "structural" relationship between the referent and the word, and a nonverbal technique of representation:

> A man desires to express the "idea of three." If he holds up three fingers, he will be understood by humans virtually anywhere on earth. But if he utters the word *three*, he will be understood only by those who know the meaning of this word. . . .
> The fingers are a symbol and so is the word; but the word is only a verbal symbol. . . . It is an *arbitrary* symbol, significant only to those familar with its arbitrary meaning. The fingers, however, are a *structurally related* symbol—they express "threeness" because they can be visually, tactually, etc., related one-to-one with any nonverbal "things." (the Map-Territory relationship). [1951, p. 16]

Note the use of capitals for the supposedly self-explanatory, now institutionalized "Map-Territory relationship." What Exton fails to acknowledge is that there may be a great many relationships between the map and the territory which are quite as arbitrary as the use of the word "three."

Students of perception and philosophy also frequently employ the map metaphor and make much of the fundamental significance of the spatial conception. Polanyi (1963) makes considerable use of maps and mapping in his discussions of knowledge and knowing. Maps are one form of what he calls *explicit knowledge*, a kind of factual reality, and as such they are subject to critical reflection, both by the person who made the map and by those who may later use it. He finds maps to be a particularly useful example, for they lend themselves easily to checking; truth may be more easily agreed upon with maps than with certain other forms of knowledge, such as writing. Such an assertion is true, of course, only of the simplest notion of getting from one place to another with the use of a map; there are other aspects of mapping—cartographic generalization, for example—which can be as elusive as anything in print. Polanyi points out that there is also a personal knowledge, or *tacit knowledge* as he calls it, which is also present whenever an individual encounters some form of explicit knowledge, such as a map. He points out that this tacit knowledge is the fundamental understanding process, and it is not available for critical surveillance as the explicit knowledge is:

> I had shown that purely tacit operations of the mind are processes of understanding; I will go further now by suggesting that the understanding of words and other symbols is also a tacit process. Words can convey information, a series of algebraic symbols can constitute a mathematical deduction, a map can set out the topography of a region; but neither words nor symbols nor maps can be said to communicate understanding of themselves. [1963, p. 21]

Hence the impossibility of using the map to explain the map.

Cassirer (1957) is concerned with the fundamental nature of the spatial experience. Of basic importance is the "symbolic concept," man's chief activity being symbol formation. This is thought to be true whether the symbols are those of language, art, history, or science. The world which man experiences is not one of raw sensations, merging perceptions, but is one mediated by a constructive, active intellect which organizes these perceptions into symbol systems. As Cassirer sees it the most fundamental organization is spatial in nature.

> In truth, however, what we call the world of our perception is not simple, not given and self-evident from the outset, but "is" only insofar as it has gone through certain basic theoretical acts by which it is apprehended and specified. This universal relationship is perhaps most evident in the intuitive form of our perceptual world, in its spatial form. The relations of "together," "separate," "side by side," are not just "given" along with our "simple" sensations, the sensuous matter that is order in space; they are a highly complex, thoroughly *mediated* product of empirical thought. When we attribute a certain size, position, and distance to things in space, we are not thereby expressing a simple datum of sensation but are situating the sensory data in a relationship and system, which proves ultimately to be nothing other than a relationship of pure judgment. [1955, 2:30]

The articulation of things in space is therefore preceded by an articulation in judgment. Differences in spatial articulation (in terms of position, size, and distance) can be grasped and assigned since the separate sensory impressions are differentiated by judgment *because* different significances are imputed to them. These concepts are not a priori in any way, but are constructed because human activity finds them significant. There is great similarity between this view and that of Piaget and Inhelder, on the development of representational space, a fact noted by Harvey (1969, pp. 192–93).

Cassirer finds that the problem of space enters all fields of knowledge, indicating to him that its pervasiveness is somehow related to the pervasiveness of symbolism. As did Piaget and Inhelder, for different reasons, Cassirer decides that representational space is a construction, a result of symbolic activity:

> . . . there is no field of philosophy or theoretical knowledge in general into which the problem of space does not in some way enter and with which it is not interwoven in one way or another. Metaphysics and epistemology, physics and psychology are all equally interested in the problem and its solution. . . . How, then, is the problem of space related to the general problem of symbolism? Is the space in which things are represented to us a simple intuitive datum, or does it follow from a process of symbolic formation? [1957, 3:143]

Cassirer concludes that the transition from experience in real space to the ability to represent space internally is a crucial one in man's intellectual development:

> Certain movements may be fixed by long practice, they may always be performed identically with the help of certain mechanisms, but this does not necessarily lead to a representative consciousness, to any representation and actualization of the separateness and succession of their different stages. There is no doubt that this transition to the pure representation of spatial relations is also a relatively late step in the development of human consciousness. Reports on primitive peoples show that their spatial orientation, though very much keener and more precise than that of civilized man, moves wholly in the channels of a concrete spatial feeling. Though every point in their surroundings, every bend in the river for example, may be exactly known to them, they will still be unable to draw a map of the river, to hold it fast in a spatial schema. The transition from mere action to the schema, to the symbol, to rep-

resentation, signifies in every case a genuine "crisis" of the
spatial consciousness; moreover it is not limited to the spatial
consciousness but goes hand in hand with a general spiritual
transformation, an authentic revolution in the mode of thinking. [1957, 3:152–53]

In Cassirer's view, spatiality is also the basis for all language
development:

The investigation of language . . . has shown us that a vast
number of the most diverse relations, particularly qualitative
and modal relations, come within the scope of language only
indirectly, by way of spatial determinations. The simple spatial
terms thus became a kind of original intellectual expression.
The objective world became intelligible to language to the
degree in which language was able, as it were, to translate it
back into terms of space. [1955, 2:85–86]

Labeling signifies an articulation of phenomena, and for any things
or impressions to be separated from the flow of ongoing existence,
there must be the separation which we call spatial. The sundering of
the "I" from "the world" is, Cassirer feels, based on a spatial
intuition:

Even where language progresses to its highest, specifically intellectual achievements—even where, instead of naming things or
attributes, occurrences or actions, it designates pure relations—
this purely significative act does not, by and large, surpass certain limits of concrete, intuitive representation. . . . Even the
terms by which language expresses the "is" of the predicative
statement usually preserve a secondary intuitive significance—
the logical relation is replaced by a spatial one, a "being-here"
or "being-there," a statement of existence . . . Language may
be said to gain its first foothold in the sphere of space, whence it
progressively extends its sway over the whole of intuitive
reality. [1957, 3:450]

Cassirer outlines a sequence of development for spatial representation which is identical to that of Piaget and Inhelder. From
elementary relations, such as near and far, in topological space, with
no particularly consistent point of view, the human gains flexibility
as he develops a conception of space which includes other points of
view, such as projective and Euclidean space.

The truly great achievement which the ability to map represents in the history of human intellectual development is pointed out in a number of ways by Cassirer (1957, vol. 3). For example, he describes the impairment of spatial representation ability in aphasic disorders. In this neurological condition, a patient may operate with reasonable facility in concrete space, but be unable to perform the integrative activity necessary to create a coherent representational space. Cassirer observes that certain patients could not draw sketches of their rooms or routes, but could orient themselves reasonably well when presented with a sketch in which the basic schema was already laid down: "Thus the truly difficult operation consists in knowing how to proceed in the spontaneous choice of a plane as well as the center of the coordinates. For precisely this choice unmistakeably involves a constructive act." A certain patient is quoted as telling why he could not draw a plan of his room: "I couldn't do it. I couldn't get the starting point. I knew where all the things were in the room, but I had difficulty in getting a starting point when it came to setting them down on a plan" (3:245). Cassirer, emphasizing the intellectual achievement in the construction of space, writes:

> We perceive the true nature of the difficulty when we consider how long it took science or theoretical knowledge to perform this same operation [choice of a point of view] with clarity and determinacy. Theoretical physics also began with "thing space" and only gradually progressed to "systematic space"—it, too, had to conquer the concept of a system and center of coordinates by persistent intellectual effort. [3:245]

The ultimate significance of the spatial concept has led to the map metaphor being widely employed in other fields. In the field of psychology, for example, the term "cognitive map" is currently much in vogue. Apparently the first psychologist to use the term was Edward Tolman (1948), and he did so at a time in the history of psychology when the breadth of his point of view was not immediately appreciated. Much attention in the field then was being devoted to stimulus-response associations, from a rather mechanistic point of view, at least in connection with animals running mazes. Tolman's conception of learning as consisting of more than just a string of simple associations was something of a major departure in the field. In very recent years, his point of view has become much more accepted, however, as has the entire field of cognitive psychology. In his article on cognitive maps, Tolman is attempting to develop theory about the behavior of rats as they learn to run mazes:

> Let us turn now to the second main school. This group (and I
> belong to them) may be called the field theorists. We believe
> that in the course of learning something like a field map of the
> environment gets established in the rat's brain . . . we assert that
> the central office itself [of the brain] is far more like a map
> control room than it is like an old-fashioned telephone
> exchange. The stimuli, which are allowed in, are not connected
> by just simple one-to-one switches to the outgoing responses.
> Rather, the incoming impulses are usually worked over and
> elaborated in the central control room into a tentative,
> cognitive-like map of the environment. [1951, p. 244]

Tolman also distinguishes between those cognitive maps which
are narrow and striplike and those which are broad and comprehensive. This distinction is surprisingly like the development of representational space in the child as outlined by Piaget and Inhelder (1967),
which involves a transition from restricted topological connections to
the greater flexibility of a comprehensive Euclidean space. Tolman,
in summary, believes that learning consists not so much of building
a series of stimulus-response connections as of developing sets in the
nervous system which function like cognitive maps. This view has
become far more popular in recent times than it was when he
proposed it. For example, Wehling and Charters observe:

> One contemporary view among psychologists is that human
> beings form representations, or cognitive maps, of the external
> world which then serve as mediators for experiencing and
> responding to reality. Psychologists' investigations in the last
> decade or so have focussed on the formal properties of these
> representations—their concreteness or abstractness, openness-
> closedness, simplicity–complexity, and the like—but few have
> sought to delineate the substance of cognitive maps in a given
> domain. [1969, p. 7]

Students of scientific methodology also employ the map as a
metaphor. The cartographer Board develops the analogy of maps as
models and concludes, "By recognizing maps as models of the real
world and by employing them as conceptual models in order
better to understand the real world, their central importance in
geographic methodology is assured" (1967, p. 719). Important
for our purposes here are the instances where models, languages,

understanding, theories of reality and so on are likened to maps. Kuhn provides a clear example of the a priori use of the map metaphor in relation to the functioning of the paradigm in science, an example that is particularly relevant to our objectives in this book:

> ... [The paradigm] functions by telling the scientist about the entities that nature does and does not contain and about the ways in which those entities behave. That information provides a map whose details are elucidated by mature scientific research. And since nature is too complex and varied to be explored at random, that map is as essential as observation and experiment to science's continuing development. Through the theories they embody, paradigms prove to be constitutive of the research activity. They are also constitutive of science in other respects, and that is now the point. In particular, our most recent examples show that paradigms provide scientists not only with a map but also with some of the directions essential for mapmaking. In learning a paradigm the scientist acquires theory, methods, and standards together usually in an inextricable mixture. [1962, p. 108]

Perhaps the most penetrating analysis of this is provided by Toulmin in his *Philosophy of Science*. In a most interesting and insight-providing chapter, "Theories and Maps," he analogizes the one to the other, explaining that he does so because "the problems of method facing the physicist and the cartographer are logically similar in important respects, and so are the techniques of representation they employ to deal with them" (1960, p. 105). While it was clearly not his primary purpose to do so, he provides analyses of the nature of maps which are not commonly encountered in cartography. Toulmin stresses the efficiency of maps, in providing more information than the set of point-observations which went into their making, in order to show that theories can behave in similar ways:

> the diagrams present all that is contained in the set of observational statements, but do so in a logically novel manner: the aggregate of discrete observations is transformed into a simple and connected picture, much as the collection of readings in a surveyor's note-book is transformed into a clear and orderly map. [p. 108]

He continues:

> This, of course, is the marvel of cartography: the fact that, from

a limited number of highly precise and well-chosen
measurements and observations, one can produce a map from
which can be read off an unlimited number of geographical
facts of almost as great a precision. [p. 111]

Toulmin finds that the selectivity which any mapmaker exercises
is similar to the degree of completeness which exists in any
particular theory in physics. In either case, there is no absolute
standard of ultimate completeness. He emphasizes that what is
recorded or theorized about is what is significant to man in a particular situation:

For we could say that the fundamental map was complete only
if it showed all the things which in that region it was the cartographer's ambition to record. Now it is always possible for
cartographers to develop fresh ambitions; the criteria of the
completeness of a map are, accordingly, at the mercy of history.
So are they with the theories of physics. [pp. 116–17]

Toulmin also makes a significant distinction between itineraries,
or route-maps, and more general maps—a distinction which nicely
parallels the stages of the development in human consciousness from
purely topological space notions (and the restrictions they impose) to
an all-points-of-view, projective, Euclidean space:

For the theories of the physical sciences differ from those of the
diagnostic and applied sciences much as maps differ from
itineraries. If the term "cause" is absent from the physical
sciences, so also a map of South Lancashire does not specifically tell us how to get to Liverpool. To a man making a map, all
routes are as good as each other. The users of the maps will not
all be going the same way, so a satisfactory map is route-
neutral: it represents the region mapped in a way which
is indifferent as between starting-points, destinations, and the
like. An itinerary, however, is specifically concerned with
particular routes, starting-points and destinations, and the
form it takes is correspondingly unlike that of a map. [p. 121]

The foregoing cursory review of the "map idea" in several disparate fields of learning provides clear evidence that the map is
something fundamental to man's cognitive makeup. Surprisingly,
non-cartographers seem to be more aware of this than cartographers, and as a matter of fact, most cartographers are probably not
aware of the basic role that students in other fields ascribe to maps

as a kind of a priori analogy for a variety of basic concepts. Many things are analyzed in terms of the map, and the reason for this seems simple enough; it goes one step back from the map itself. While a map itself exists and occupies space, it derives its meaning and usefulness from the fact that it represents some other space. There is fairly widespread philosophical agreement, which certainly accords with common sense, that the spatial aspects of all existence are fundamental. Before an awareness of time, there is an awareness of relations in space, and space seems to be that aspect of existence to which most other things can be analogized or with which they can be equated.

There also appears to be something appealingly simple about the "map idea," but because it seems so often to have been taken for granted, its fundamental character remains obscure. The hazy notions of structure, of topological and Euclidean relations, of the importance of an organization of space, all seem to be parts of the central but elusive *concept* called "map." In contrast, the "real" map—that produced by the cartographer—is something that is a great deal more concrete: one can look at it and touch it. Nevertheless, because it obviously involves the concept of space in the ways in which we have seen that others use that term, the material map is fundamentally just as elusive. This book is an attempt to understand the tangible map and to elaborate its cognitive significance. To do this we must develop some precise terminology, and we shall turn next to the definitions of a few limited terms needed to explore this subject.

We shall begin with the word "map," and start by examining the utility and variety of actual maps as documents. It is obvious that maps have tremendous utility, but it seems all but impossible to make an exhaustive list of the uses to which maps may be put. Many people have tried. Such inventories usually point out that a map can be a popular and scholarly tool which aids in perceiving and understanding geographical relationships; that it is an efficient means for storing spatially-anchored data; and that it is a technical device permitting easy recovery of distance, direction, and areal measurements. As a scholarly tool it serves a multitude of purposes, such as making possible inferences about the occurrence of unobserved or unobservable data, and aiding in the development and testing of spatial hypotheses (Salichtchev and Berliant 1973). The list can go on almost indefinitely. Maps can serve these functions in less sophisticated ways, as in the form of the common road map, or in highly complex ways, as in an isarithmic map of population potential. In the past maps have sometimes functioned as graphic, spatial–allegorical, didactic tools, as for example in the religious cartography of the Middle Ages. Maps even serve as ornaments. To list the variety of uses of maps and then to attempt to categorize the listing would be like attempting the same thing with a number or language system. The quantity of utilitarian permutations that are possible with words, numbers, or map marks is unlimited, for all practical purposes. In the map, then, we seem to be dealing with something clearly fundamental, something which has nearly unrestricted potential utility.

Thus, since the map is so basic and has such a multiplicity of uses, the variety of its occurrences is vast. There are specific maps and general maps, maps for the historian, for the meteorologist, for the sociologist, and so on without limit. Anything that can be spatially conceived can be mapped—and probably has been. Maps range in size from those on billboards or projection screens to postage stamps, and they may be monochrome or multicolored, simple or complex. They need not be flat—a globe is a map; they need not be of earth—there are maps of Mars and the moon; or for that matter, they need not be of anyplace real—there have been numerous maps made of imaginary "places" such as Utopia and even of the "Territory of Love" (Post 1973).

The more one contemplates the variety of the map in its forms, its versatility, and its fundamental nature, the more one is impressed with the fact that a general definition of a map must be based on its being simply a representation of things in space; *representation* and *space* are the two critical elements. We shall deal at some length with the conception of space in a later chapter, but here we need to consider briefly what kind of space is the accepted domain of the tangible map. Similarly, we need to look into the nature of the possible representations of that space in order to limit our concern to that which is appropriately called a map.

"Space" is a word with a large range of meanings: the expanse containing the solar system and stars, as well as an interval of time or the distance between two points. In order to use the concept of space in our discussion it is necessary to identify the kind of space the cartographer's map represents. Clearly, the space represented by a tangible map normally refers to the three-dimensional field of our experience; this is referred to in various ways by using such terms as "area," "territory," "region," "section of the earth," and so on.

These terms imply a limited extent of land, but often something more. For example, "territory" properly applies to a segment of the earth, but in lay language it also connotes some kind of proprietorship; but maps are neither limited necessarily to a particular segment nor even to the earth. To a geographical sophisticate the term "region" has a specialized meaning. Since maps are not limited to earth, one cannot use such terms as "section of the earth." The word "environment" could be employed because a map of a "real" area always includes the conception of the maker in one way or another, and hence the mapped section is a part of his environment. Unfortunately, for our purposes, the term "environment" has come to have such aspatial ecological overtones that it too seems inappropriate. The most general terms are probably "place" and "area"— simply a portion of space. They are quite impersonal, though, and because of the involvement of the cartographer in a map, they leave something to be desired. It is our view that the word "milieu" best connotes one's surroundings or environment in addition to its meaning of place, and thus involves the cartographer. Our definition of a map then, would be "a representation of the milieu." This leaves only the meaning of "representation" to be clarified.

To represent is to stand for, symbolize, depict, portray, present clearly to the mind, describe, and so on, and seems to occasion no problem in meaning; but what of the form that the representation takes? In spite of the fact that we use the term "numerical map" for an orderly array of numbers referring to the milieu, it seems necessary for our purposes here to put forward the proposition that a map is a graphic thing made of marks of various kinds. Traditionally, a map itself is a space in which marks that have been assigned meanings are placed in positions relative to one another in such a way that not only the marks, but also the positions and the spatial relationships among the elements, have meaning. It is thus a graphic or visual construct, and it follows that one must be able to *see* a map. Of course, there will always be the figurative use of the term, as for example in "numerical map," but for something to be a real map it must be a graphic thing that is visible, such as paper with marks on it or the fluorescence of a cathode ray tube. Presumably one may "see" a "mental map" with his "inward eye" (Gould and White 1974), but that does not negate the proposition that the map is a visual thing.

Our definition of a map turns out to be deceptively simple. "A map is a graphic representation of the milieu" does no violence to the English-language definition of a map that appears in the *Multilingual Dictionary of Technical Terms in Cartography* of Commission II of the International Cartographic Association (ICA) (Meynen 1973): "A map is a representation normally to scale and on a flat medium, of a selection of material or abstract features on, or in relation to, the surface of the Earth or of a celestial body." Our own definition strikes us as being more general. The ICA definition includes one element that is specifically and intentionally missing from ours, namely an indication of the medium employed or the form the representation usually takes.

Having defined the term "map," it would appear logical to turn next to the concept expressed by the words "mapmaker" or "cartographer." But a more fundamental label takes priority: the term "mapper." The considerable analytical work in what is called "cognitive mapping" makes it clear that humans and some other creatures appear to process some forms of sensory input such that information obtained from the milieu is arranged or converted so that they can operate as if there were an internal space like a map (Downs and Stea 1973b). In our view, whatever it is that actually occurs, this is the phenomenon that makes one a mapper. Creatures that have an elevated eye level and the mental capacity to arrange what they see into some sort of spatial framework are all potential mappers. Such an assertion covers a wide range from the high-flying eagle to the darting dragonfly to no longer earthbound man. The eyes may range from the binocular equipment of the whole man to the "vision" in the fingertips of the blind, but the essential sine qua non of the mapper is the ability to operate in a spatial mode. At the minimum this is two-dimensional (x, y) and at the maximum it is three-dimensional (x, y, z), with the possibility of some sort of integration of time as a fourth dimension (Lundberg 1973), but the spatial framework must exist as part of the cognitive endowment of the mapper. Nothing else is really essential.

It should be apparent from the foregoing that by the term "mapper" we do not mean specifically the cartographer, surveyor, geometer, photogrammetrist, and so on. Instead we refer simply to anyone who actively conceives of spatial relationships in the milieu, whether those relationships involve the hills and valleys of the topographer, the familiar nodes and corridors of the city dweller, or the invisible shoals and reefs of the ship's pilot. The conception of things in spatial relationship is the critical operation, and he who does it is a mapper. An engineer may measure the positions of objects with respect to one reference system, and a cartographer may assign diminutive graphic surrogates to those objects and position them in some other reference system to produce the tangible thing we call a map; but the mapper is the one who develops the mental construct. It really makes no difference whether he obtains his conception of the milieu by simply observing nature at scale, by looking at a map, by plotting observed items at reduced scale on some handy medium, or by compiling items from a variety of other such plottings. The mapmaker and the map viewer are, therefore, both mappers in this broad sense of the term.

Questions naturally arise regarding the nature of the spatial conception of the milieu which forms in the mind of the mapper. We have defined the map as a graphic representation, to distinguish it from verbal and numerical representations, but what does the term "map" mean with respect to the cognitive map? Are there lines and points or is it restricted to shapes defined by surfaces and edges? Are things in color? Can the mapper transform in rotation and scale at will? How sophisticated can he become with practice? Are people, as potential mappers, largely alike or quite dissimilar? And so on. Many such questions cannot be answered with our present-day knowledge, but the questions are obviously significant (Downs and Stea 1973a). Through the work of Piaget and his associates we know something of the child's conception of space; we surmise that navigators in the South Pacific conceive of position in a framework of wave patterns; the desert traveler and the Eskimo define distances in terms of travel time rather than linear extent; we have some insight into mental spatial conceptions from such studies as Lynch (1960) and those who followed his pattern (Kates 1970); but we really know very little about the cognitive map of the mapper.

Although we shall deal more specifically later in the book with the problem of the conception of space and the nature of the mental construct of the mapper, we can assert here that the cognitive map is best termed an image. Naturally the mapper's image—his personal, meaningful, mental, spatial conception of the milieu—will be a function of his past experience and his ability to involve himself in a spatial framework. Therefore, it will vary from person to person; one can confidently assert that the images of no two mappers are alike, and that the same milieu can be mapped in different ways by the same mapper.

It would be easy to confuse the concept of mapper, as here outlined, and mapmaker, because in a very real sense a mapmaker is a mapper. But in our definition of mapper we have specifically restricted the map he develops to an image which is not tangible, that is, it does not materially exist to be touched and seen by another. On the other hand, the map made by a mapmaker we define as being corporeal, and in common parlance, the terms mapmaker and cartographer are essentially synonymous.

Among those who are concerned with the preparation and production of maps (charts) a rather careful distinction is generally drawn between mapping in the sense of mapmaking on the one hand and cartography on the other. "Mapping" refers to all the operations involved in the production of a tangible map. Because the terms "map" and "chart" refer to all kinds of maps—from the large-scale, general topographic map of a land surface and the nautical chart on the one hand to the specialized thematic map on the other—the contributory activities range along a spectrum from geodetic survey and position-finding, through various kinds of compilation, generalization, and decision-making, to the construction of the artwork for the printer at the far end, with myriad technical procedures and executions in between. The term "cartography" is generally restricted to that portion of the operation often termed "creative," that is, concerned with the design of the map, "design" being used here in a broad sense to involve all the major decision-making having to do with specification of scale, projection, symbology, typography, color, and so on. The cartographer must therefore be, among other things, part mathematician, part production expert, part student of graphic semiology, and part geographer. To use a literary parallel, his is the critical role equivalent to that of an author. Usually when we employ the terms "cartographer" or "mapmaker" we will be using them in this sense of "author." Naturally a cartographer must be a mapper in the sense of our definition of that term, but it is evident that a mapper need not be a mapmaker.

As is apparent from the preceding, "mapper" is the all-inclusive term encompassing all who increase their spatial knowledge of the milieu by any sort of sensory input. As we have suggested, this input can range from the visual observation of the milieu directly or indirectly (as by use of aerial photographs), to verbal statements, to measurement with instruments, to looking at an already-made map. Even the blind person feeling his way around a room and the flying bat in the dark with his built-in radar are mappers in this sense.

This book is specifically concerned with the mapper whose sensory input is limited to the tangible map and the complex relations among himself, the map, and the milieu. For this reason, it is necessary to employ a term which specifically denotes the particular mapper who augments his spatial knowledge of the milieu as a consequence of looking at a map. For this we shall use the simple term "percipient."* The (map) percipient, one who obtains information about the milieu by looking at a map, is coordinate with the cartographer, one who attempts to communicate spatial information about the milieu by making a map.

The use of the term "percipient" makes it possible to distinguish those who, by looking at a map, add to their fund of spatial knowledge or acquire additional meaning, from those we designate by the more restricted terms "map reader" and "map user." The term "map reading" implies a rather specific and limited action, such as looking up the name of a city or country, or finding out how high a particular hill is. Similarly, the term "map user" connotes the employment of a map for a specific purpose, such as that of the farmer who obtains the data needed for contour plowing, or the engineer who lays out a road with the help of soil and topographic maps. Neither the map reader nor the map user is necessarily adding to his spatial knowledge. Both terms suggest operations similar to that of using a dictionary to find out simply how to spell or pronounce a word, which adds little if anything to one's understanding of the meaning of the word and therefore of the language to which it belongs.

The authors believe that although the concept of the map is thought by many students to be of fundamental significance, the nature of the map as an image and the manner in which it functions as a communication device between the cartographer and the percipient need much deeper consideration and analysis than they

*The term "percipient" is a generally accepted appelation employed by those who study perception. For several years the authors used the term "cartoleger" (kar-tol'-ə-jər), but decided against employing it in this book mainly to escape the accusation of creating jargon. "Cartoleger" has etymological justification: "cart" is from F *carte* map, fr. L *charta*, Gk *khartes* sheet, leaf; "leg" is from L *legere*, Gk *legein* gather, speak, choose, read, cf. "legend," "legible." In French "cartoleger" would be *"cartolège,"* and in German *"Kartoleg,"* coordinate with *"cartographe"* and *"Kartograph."* A natural cognate of "cartoleger" would be "cartology," the study of the map as a medium of communication and has been proposed in the literature (Ratajski 1970; 1973, pp. 220–226). "Cartology" has the obvious advantages of simplicity and a readily apparent meaning over another term sometimes used, "metacartography." "Cartology" has also been suggested several times as a term to cover the study of maps as documents (their origins, history, quality, etc.), but it has not been generally accepted.

have yet received. Part of the reason for this deficiency is that until recently the emphasis in cartography has been restricted largely to the map itself. Cartographers are frequently engaged—on deadline—in producing maps for immediate consumption in protecting the environment or fighting the expressway traffic. The maps they make work well enough, most of the time. But there is a need in cartography for another point of view, an analysis from someplace other than the production line. It seems that too often meaning can be obtained from the map only with great effort and annoyance, or with an amazing loss of information between cartographer and percipient. There has not been, in the field of cartography, a thorough delineation of the methodological and philosophical bases on which an analysis of the acquisition and transmission of spatial knowledge via the map could be conducted.

Such an analysis clearly must deal with more than just the physical characteristics of the map. It must probe the characteristics of human beings as they see and know, spatially, and how they use maps to understand and communicate this knowledge. The emphasis must shift from the map as a static graphic display to the cognitive and perceptual activities of the individuals who interact with maps, namely, those mappers who are mapmakers or map percipients. Such a study leads us inevitably into the broad field of psychology, but also into aspects of philosophy, epistemology, and other fields as well. This is a large order. To be sure, there have been systems analysts, researchers in human engineering, and some psychologists who have conducted inquiries into one aspect or another of map design and use. But the problem as a whole seems to need and deserve a great deal more thoughtful attention. So far a broad research paradigm specific to the field of cartography has not emerged from the fragmentary research activity.

For the most part, up to this time, the psychological research which has been conducted in connection with cartography and percipients has been carried on with the methodologic assumptions of the field of behavioral psychology, as, for example, in psychophysical studies which attempt to measure and compare stimulus and response magnitudes. Some of this material has proved quite useful in some practical mapmaking situations, but its applicability has been restricted. Furthermore, its capacity for generalization is severely limited, and thus it has furnished little basis for prediction in new applications in cartography.

The authors feel strongly the need for a more general research

paradigm, but that is a lofty objective which involves very fundamental considerations. We find it necessary to turn to the ideas and
terminology of other academic fields for assistance in understanding
our own. We must come to terms with what constitutes "meaning"
in our own field of cartography–geography. We must draw on the
work of others for some insight into the nature of the human being
as learner and knower, particularly about things spatial. For
example, we find that we become very heavily indebted to Piaget and
his co-workers for the understanding of the conception of space and
articulation within it. Moreover, we owe much to the writings of
Polanyi for a grasp of the difference between tacit and explicit
knowledge, and for his very lucid analysis of part-whole relationships and the nature of meaning. Conversely, we shall examine
studies of cartographic communication and information theory, in
the next chapter, only to find that they are not of much help in our
probe for the theoretical foundations of cartography. We shall
consider particularly the map–language analogy—ultimately, however, to discard it.

We hope that in the various comparisons of maps with other
things, this point does not become obscured: maps are both *unique*
and *fundamental*. All of the subsequent chapters deal with critical
aspects of communication, cognition, space, human characteristics,
and so on, in order that we may better understand what it is that
makes maps so exceptional.

2 The Map as a Communication System

The very best map-reader has to suffer some shocks when he comes face to face with reality.

Josephine Tey

Just as most writing assumes a reader, most mapmaking assumes a map percipient, a viewer to whom the map will convey information. The author–reader transfer and the cartographer–map percipient transfer are each systems of communication. They differ in essential ways, however, as noted by Moles (1964) and Bertin (1968, 1970). As we shall see in the next chapter, the differences between mapping and language are such that the two systems of communication have markedly different cognitive characteristics. At this point in our analysis of cartography, however, we are concerned only with the nature of the system in which the map is the medium of communication between the cartographer on the one hand and the map percipient on the other. It is important that we examine the character of this system for two reasons. One is to determine the basic characteristics of the communication process as it operates in cartography, since one can hardly employ a method efficiently unless its essential attributes are understood. The other, and much the more important for our purpose, is to see whether the investigations made so far into cartographic communication have advanced the theoretical underpinnings of the field to any significant extent.

When one surveys the history of cartographic thought he cannot help but be surprised at the fact that, until recently, very little concern, either practical or theoretical, has been focused on the map as a communication system. Koláčný summarized this state of affairs:

> In fact, however, cartographic theory and practice have almost exclusively been concerned with the creation and production of cartographic works, so far. One would hardly believe how little thought literature has until recently given to the theory and practice of map using. Not until in the last few years have the authors of some handbooks complemented their definitions of cartography by extending the term to the employment of maps.

On the present level of cartographic theory and practice, the work of the map user is therefore largely determined by the cartographer's product. There prevails the tacit assumption that the user will simply learn to work with any map which the cartographer makes. In other words, the map user is expected to submit, more or less, to the cartographer's conditions. [1968, p. 1]

Only since the burgeoning of cartography in the 1940s has the percipient—that is, the receiver of the information prepared by the cartographer—become a subject for investigation. Earlier general analyses such as those of Robinson (1952) and Keates (1962), and more specific psychophysical investigations into stimulus-response relationships (Flannery [1956], Williams [1956], Clarke [1959], Ekman, Lindman, and William-Olsson [1961], and Jenks and Knos [1961]) dealt primarily with particular characteristics of the map percipient. This explicit concern with the reactions of the viewer to the graphic components of the map was not, of course, the beginning of such interest. Occasionally, earlier cartographers had wondered about the effectiveness of what they did, but that interest was not considered a part of cartography. It was not until the development of formal communication theory and investigation into information processing systems that cartography incorporated this aspect. In his review of the subject and method of cartography, Salichtchev (1970, pp. 84–85) remarks on the "strong ties [that] have emerged between cartography and the theory of scientific information," and he incorporates "the theory and methods of map use" as one of the elements comprising the content of contemporary cartography.

A review of the literature of cartography during the past two decades reveals a persistent increase in the concern for the problems of cartographic communication. Numerous master's theses and some doctoral dissertations have been concerned with facets of the broad subject, varying from the general, which range over the entire system (e.g., Dornbach 1967) to the specific, in which selected elements of the map are examined (e.g., R. D. Wright 1967; Pearson 1970; Dent 1971; Cuff 1972). Published research which relates various characteristics of the percipient to specific questions of cartographic design has appeared regularly, such as Castner and Robinson (1969); Crawford (1971); Flannery (1971); Dent (1972); Head (1972); Cuff (1973); and Meihoefer (1973). Special sessions at meetings of cartographic organizations as well as separate symposia dealing with problems of cartographic design in relation to the intended use of maps have proliferated, and in 1972 the General Assembly of the International Cartographic Association created Commission V, Communication in Cartography (Ratajski 1974, p. 140), with the following terms of reference:

1. The elaboration of basic principles of map language
2. The evaluation of both the effectiveness and efficiency of communication by means of maps with reference to the different groups of map users
3. The theory of cartographic communication, i.e. the transmission of information by means of maps.

Numerous attempts to enlist the aid of information theory have been reported, a subject to be dealt with explicitly later in this chapter. All in all, there seems no doubt that the field of cartography has opened wide its arms to welcome the concept that it is a communication system. To be sure, there are always those who recoil from such things as being theoretical and impractical ("let's get on with the job of making maps"), but it is doubtful that the trend can be resisted. The dean of European cartographers, Eduard Imhof, stated it clearly and vigorously in a closing section of *Kartographische Geländedarstellung* dealing with the Reform of Map Graphics:

> A good part of the labors of topographers and map editors remains fruitless because of graphic defects. A very important user of graphics once condemned maps simply as "graphic outrages." It is in order, therefore, to clean out the Augean stables. Many excellent cartographers have already begun this Sisyphean [-like] task. *Map graphics must be reformed.* Only the simple is strongly expressive. A map should contain nothing that a normally gifted user cannot easily see. The "laws of vision" and the experience of map readers are to be followed and observed. [1965, p. 400]

As an accomplished artist and teacher, Imhof lays great stress on good training and gifted personnel, but it seems fully as important that the cartographer clearly understand his role in the larger system of communication of which he is but one part.

One may study communication systems in several ways. At one end of the range is the attempt to model the organization simply on the basis of the energy inputs, flows, and losses in the various parts of the system. At the other extreme one can attempt to analyze the information content itself and the relation between the substantive input and the output of the system. Most analyses of the mapping communication system will incorporate some aspects of both and will thus lie somewhere between the extremes. We will begin our analysis of the cartographic communication system by first looking at the simplest possible form of a general communication network.

Singh (1966) shows that a typical communications network consists fundamentally of a source (or transmitter), a channel which conveys the message, and a receiver (Fig. 2.1). In everyday terms a speaking person would be the source, the air which carries the sound waves of his voice would be the channel, and a listener would be the receiver. A more detailed analysis of the basic system will usually include the insertion of an encoder between the source and the channel and a decoder between the channel and the receiver, so that the system will be as diagrammed in Fig. 2.2. The function of the encoder is to improve the efficiency of the system. In our original analogy the voice mechanism of the speaker constitutes the encoder, taking the thoughts of the source and transforming them into sound waves, while the hearing mechanism of the listener is the decoder, transforming the sound waves back into thoughts. The elements of other systems, such as telegraphy, the hand-sign language of the deaf, television, and so on, are easy to fit into the same sort of model.

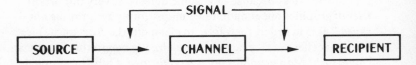

Fig. 2.1. Fundamentals of a communication system

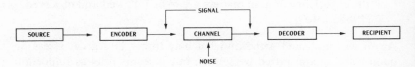

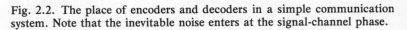

Fig. 2.2. The place of encoders and decoders in a simple communication system. Note that the inevitable noise enters at the signal-channel phase.

An unwanted but apparently inevitable component of every communication system is the element called "noise." Noise consists of interference with the signal, such as incorrect voice sounds in speech, static in radio, and distortions of appearance in television. In the modeling of the general communication system the noise is shown as entering the system at the channel (signal) phase (Fig. 2.2). As we shall see later, the concept of noise is considerably more elusive in the cartographic communication system.

With a little squeezing and broad analogy the cartographic communication process can also be made to resemble the generalized communication system. For example, Board (1967, pp. 672-75), in his discussion of the map/model analogy, employs the following generalized communication system drawn from Johnson and Klare. Board makes use of a map which shows on a nominal scale the occurrence of the older "ridge and furrow" cultivation patterns in the Midland counties of England. Board likens the source (Fig. 2.3) to the real world, the encoding to the black symbolism on the map employed to show the presence of ridge and furrow, the signal to the graphic pattern provided by the black patches and blocks, the receiver to the eyes of the reader of the *Geographical Journal* in which the map appeared, and the decoder to the mind of the reader who is, of course, the destination. No transmitter is indicated and noise is assumed to be "distracting information," a component not identified, but by implication consisting of anything other than the primary signal, and which thus presumably includes "essential names and insets," although how anything can be both essential and noise is not made clear.

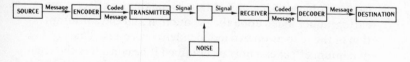
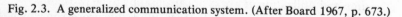

Fig. 2.3. A generalized communication system. (After Board 1967, p. 673.)

It was not Board's purpose to investigate the degree of correspondence between the cartogaphic system and the general model of communication systems, but the example shows that clearly they are similar. The world and the cartographer constitute the source, the map is the coded "message," the signal is made up of the "light waves" which make the message visible, the channel is space, and the receiver, decoder, and destination are the eyes and mind of the recipient. Nevertheless, as Board and others realize, when the cartographic communication process is analyzed in detail it is evident that it departs significantly from the general model.

The general model simply assumes a given message, its transmission, and its receipt. Any specialized system, such as the cartographic, will incorporate complex processes of selection and interpretation in both the source (the cartographer) and the destination (the percipient). These, along with whatever corresponds to noise in the general system, produce a discrepancy between the real world on the one hand and the image developed by the percipient on the other. Part of this difference is due to the personalized, and therefore inevitably "distorted," views of reality held by the cartographer and by the percipient; part is due to the methods of coding the message, i.e., the map made by the cartographer and its decoding by the percipient. To reduce this discrepancy is, of course, a fundamental aim in cartography.

The first step in this direction is the realization that the mapmaker and the percipient are not independent of one another, and that an increase in the efficiency of the system depends upon an active feedback, so to speak, from the decoding, percipient phase, to the encoding, mapmaking phase. This was clearly realized in the earliest penetrating analysis of the problem made by Koláčný (1968). This stemmed from an elaborate research program on various aspects of the efficiency of cartographic symbolism carried out at the Research Institute for Geodesy and Cartography in Prague during the period 1959–68. Koláčný reported:

> cartographic work cannot obtain its maximum effect if the cartographer looks upon the production and the consumption of the map as on two independent processes. That maximum effect can only be obtained if he considers the creation and utilization of works of cartography to be two components of a coherent and in a sense indivisible process in which cartographical information originates, is communicated and produces an effect . . .
>
> The creation and communication of cartographic information is actually a very complex process of activities and operations with feedback circuits on various levels. [1968, pp. 3–4]

To illustrate this basic system Koláčný constructed a diagram—shown here in simplified form—(Fig. 2.4), which has been often reproduced (e.g., Koláčný 1968, p. 9; Koláčný 1970, p. 180;

Woodward 1974, p. 104). His identification of the basic components is as follows (1968, p. 4):

> U_1-reality (the Universe) represented as seen by the cartograper;
> S_1 -the subject representing reality, i.e. the cartographer;
> L -cartographic language as a system of map symbols and rules for their use;
> M -the product of cartography, i.e. the map;
> S_2 -the subject consuming the map, i.e. the map user [percipient];
> U_2-reality (the Universe) as seen by the map user; and
> I_c -cartographic information.

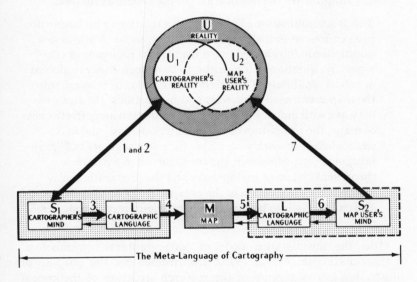

Fig. 2.4. A simplified version of Koláčný's diagram of cartographic communication. (After Koláčný 1968.)

Koláčný characterized the individual stages in the process, as numbered on Fig. 2.4 as follows:

> 1. Selective observation of polydimensional geographical reality, U_1 [the milieu], by the cartographer with specific objectives in mind.
> 2. Development of a concept of the milieu by the cartographer.

3. Transformation of the selected polydimensional geographical information into a two-dimensional intellectual model.
4. Preparation of a map in which the two-dimensional model is "objectified" by employing map symbols.
5. Production of an informative effect upon the percipient in which the mapped information transforms his earlier conception of reality.
6. Creation in the mind of the percipient of what is, to him, a new polydimensional model of U, namely U_1, the conception held by the cartographer.
7. Employment, directly or indirectly, of the new conception by the recipient.

Koláčný summarizes the implications of the system as follows:

> This is a combination of very complex relations which have not been conceived in their mutual relations, so far. Various new questions are thus added to the traditional problems of cartography, questions which hitherto have been either neglected or solved separately. This refers in particular to research into the map user's needs, interests and inclinations, the study of his work with maps, the check on the function and effectiveness of maps, the promotion of "map-consciousness" and of desirable habits of work with maps, the encouragement of "map-fancying," etc. Moreover, the construction of a complete theoretical system of cartography and the preparation of methods for the solution of the prospective tasks of cartography also call for light to be shed on the problems mentioned. [1968, p. 7]

Much the most detailed model of "cartographical transmission" is that of Ratajski (1972, 1973). Constructed for the purpose of illustrating his conception of the research structure of theoretical cartography, it is very similar in essentials to the model of Koláčný. Rather like a diagrammatic plan of an urban mass transportation system, it charts the routes of transmission and characterizes them in terms of input and output, as well as their efficiency. Like Koláčný, Ratajski makes no attempt to analyze the fundamental nature of the percept itself other than to observe that the map is a product of selective observation and symbolization of reality. The map, when observed by a "receiver (map user)," results in an "imagination of reality" more or less at variance with reality because of losses in information and in efficiency occasioned by a variety of factors including the input of both the cartographer and the percipient. It is to be expected that both Koláčný's and Ratajski's formulations of the transmission of cartographic information will be generally accepted as basic outlines of the essentials of the communication process in cartography; Salichtchev has already so employed Koláčný's in simplified fashion (Salichtchev 1973a, 1973b; Woodward 1974).

Others have found it useful to simplify the model of cartographic communication to focus attention on either the mechanics involved or the substantive characteristics. Muehrcke (1969, p. 3; 1970, pp. 199–200) characterizes the cartographic process as a series of transformations, and he diagrams their relationship (Fig. 2.5). His description of the process is as follows:

> Data are selected from the real world (T_1), the cartographer transforms these data into a map (T_2), and information is retrieved from the map through an interpretive reading process (T_3). A measure of the communication efficiency of the cartographic process is related to the amount of transmitted information, which is simply a measure of the correlation between input and output information. The cartographer's task is to devise better and better approximations to a transformation, T_2, such that output from T_3 is equal to input to T_2; i.e., $T_3 = T_2^{-1}$. [1970, p. 199]

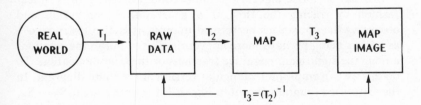

Fig. 2.5. Muehrcke's diagram of the cartographic processing system

Muehrcke's model points up clearly the important activities in cartography. Each of the transformations is an appropriate area for research and development and provides a useful framework into which to fit these activities. Muehrcke himself has so employed it with respect to thematic cartography (1972), but no such review has been undertaken in the area of nonthematic general mapping, although there have been a few significant studies such as the penetrating analysis by Keates (1972) of the shortcomings of the transformation of real-world facts to the generalized symbolism of topographic maps.

Instead of concentrating attention on the operational aspects of cartography, so to speak, as Muehrcke did, one can focus on the substantive aspects employing some of the stages of Koláčný (1968) and Ratajski (1972), but in a simplified manner. If we diagram this, we obtain the array shown in Fig. 2.6. This comes much closer to the idealized information-processing system discussed at the beginning of this chapter, in the sense that the cartographer's (selective) conception of the real world (C_2) is the message to be transmitted, the map (C_3) is the coded signal, and percipient's conception (C_4) is the message received. The arrows connecting the stages constitute Muehrcke's transformations.

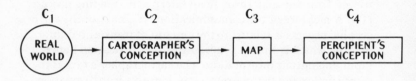

Fig. 2.6. A diagram of the cartographic communication system, with emphasis upon the conceptual aspects.

Instead of modeling cartographic communication in a linear fashion by tracing the flow of a geographical conception and observing the operations performed upon it, it is also instructive— as well as being perhaps more appropriate—to "map" the relations among the significant cognitive fractions of the communication. To do this we can employ a rectangular version of the Venn diagram. In the simplified diagram shown in Fig. 2.7, the entire area, $S_c + S_e$, represents the total conception of the geographical milieu held by mankind, A represents one cartographer's conception or image of a subset of that milieu, and B, another subset, comprises the image of the milieu held by a percipient-to-be of a map prepared by the cartographer. The dashed line separating S_c and S_e divides the conception of the milieu into error-free (S_c) and erroneous (S_e) segments. The definition of what constitutes error in this context need not now concern us. The relative sizes of A and B in the diagram symbolize an assumption that the cartographer has a more extended image of the milieu than the percipient, a generally desirable state of affairs but also immaterial to our purpose here. Both A and B are coincident for a portion of S, showing that the images held by the cartographer and the percipient are the same in some respects.

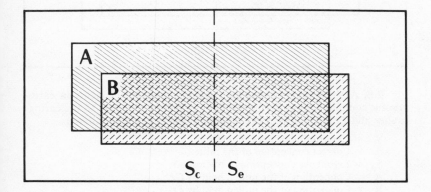

Fig. 2.7. A Venn diagram symbolizing man's conception of the geographical milieu. Diagram elements are as follows:

S_c = Correct conception of the milieu
S_e = Erroneous conception of the milieu
A = A cartographer's conception of the milieu
B = A percipient's conception of the milieu

In Fig. 2.8 the shaded rectangle, M, superimposed on Fig. 2.7 symbolizes the conception of the milieu put in the graphic form of a map by a cartographer. It is the "coded message" in the general communication system previously discussed. The rectangle, M, lies on both sides of the dashed line separating the error-free from the erroneous conceptions of the milieu: it is reasonable to assume that any map will contain some component of error arising not only from incorrect conceptions of the milieu but from error introduced by the cartographer or percipient.

The area of M is composed of three subdivisions: M_1, M_2, and M_3. The first, M_1, represents a kind of redundant fraction of the map consisting of that information which was already a part of the percipient's understanding. In other words, M_1 added nothing— for example, a first-rate geographer would ordinarily find nothing new

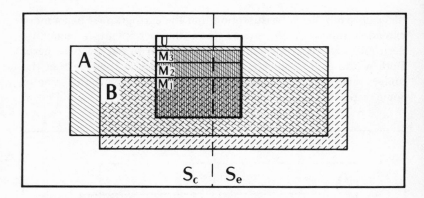

Fig. 2.8. A Venn diagram summarizing the cognitive elements in carto-graphic communication. In the terminology below, *Cr* refers to the cartog-rapher and *Pt* to the percipient. Diagram elements are as follows:

S   = Geographical space, the milieu
S_c = Correct conception of the milieu
S_e = Erroneous conception of the milieu
A   = Conception of the milieu held by *Cr*
B   = Conception of the milieu held by *Pt*
M   = Map prepared by *Cr* and viewed by *Pt*
M_1 = Fraction of M previously conceived by *Pt*
M_2 = Fraction of M not previously conceived by *Pt*
         and newly comprehended by him: an indirect
         increment
M_3 = Fraction of M not comprehended by *Pt*
U   = Increase in conception of S by *Pt* not directly
         portrayed by M but which occurs as a conse-
         quence of M: an indirect increment

to him in an outline map of the United States. The fraction M_2 symbolizes those elements included in the map not previously comprehended by the percipient and thus constitutes a direct increment to his spatial understanding. The portion M_3 represents the fraction of M not comprehended by the percipient; accordingly, it symbolizes the discrepancy between input and output in the communication system. This breakdown in the information transfer can occur for many reasons, but whatever the causes may be, it is a matter of critical concern to cartography. This has been recognized by cartographers who have studied the process (Board 1967, pp. 682–83, 698–704; Koláčný 1968; Muehrcke 1969, pp. 2–5; Muehrcke

1972, p. 3), but generally speaking no systematic study of the deficiency represented by M_3 has as yet been undertaken, mainly because the investigation of why something does not occur is a task that is both never-ending and unrewarding. One element contributing to the discrepancy between input and output in the cartographic system is the noise presumed to be present. Although the *term* is widely used, it is not easy to comprehend the *concept*.

The unwanted signals that enter an electronic communications system, such as static in radio or humming in a telephone, came to be called noise for obvious reasons. When broadcasting systems added a graphic dimension, it was only natural for the electronically produced snow on a television screen also to be called noise. The term is now widely used to refer to anything in a graphic display that interferes with the percipient obtaining the desired message. There is, however, a marked difference between the concepts of electronic noise and of graphic noise, assuming each must be a part of that which is perceived. A radio blaring close at hand while one is trying to talk on the telephone may be noisy, but it is not noise in the communication system. Consequently, those deterrents to graphic communication, such as a severe headache or external distractions, which interfere with the percipient's concentration are not properly called noise because they are not a part of the system. But even here one gets on shaky ground: it is difficult to assert that one's head, even an aching one, is not part of the system.

Generally, when one refers to the graphic noise inhibiting cartographic communication, one points the finger at a variety of distracting elements, such as unduly prominent patterns, eye-catching configurations, dense or overpowering lettering, or simultaneous contrasts of hue and value (cf. Merriam's "eye noise," 1970). There is an almost unlimited number of such occurrences which can qualify as graphic obfuscations, but they are not easy to define and classify. When an odd geographical shape, or any other element difficult to see past, draws the eye but is part of that which is being communicated, it is illogical to call the same thing both message and noise in the same situation. To define noise as simply that which the percipient finds graphically distracting would be unsatisfactory because it ignores the message component. It is not our purpose here to define noise, but it does seem reasonable in analogy with the original meaning of the term, to suggest that graphic noise may have to be limited to those delineations that are not necessary to the communication of the message. In any case, it is a significant part of the deficiency represented by M_3 in Fig. 2.8.

Two other sections of M in Fig. 2.8 symbolize additional consequences of the preparation and perception of a map. The area designated as U represents an increase in spatial understanding by the percipient that may occur because of his viewing the map—an increase in understanding which was neither intended nor symbolized in any way by the cartographer. For example, if the percipient were quite familiar with the bedrock structure of a mapped area and the map showed the surface hydrography of the region, including the occurrence of springs, the existence of a significant correlation between spring frequency and the intersection of the ground surface with the contact between pervious and impervious beds might well come to mind, although this relationship is not actually mapped. Area U signifies a kind of unplanned increment, and it is probably a fairly common occurrence for geographically sophisticated percipients who integrate the limited symbolization of the milieu on a map with their previously acquired understanding.

The areas of M and U in Fig. 2.8 which fall in the region of S_e stand for a significant *negative* component. Collectively they represent the "error term" in the cartographer–percipient equation. The error can occur simply as a consequence of "normal" incorrect conceptions of the milieu—things that might arise, for example, because of instrumental and observational error in data gathering or processing, or as a consequence of symbolism (J. K. Wright 1942; Blumenstock 1953; Robinson and Sale 1969). As a specific example, numerous studies, such as those of Flannery (1956; 1971), Clarke (1959), Ekman, Lindman, and William-Olsson (1961), and many others have clearly shown that, when graduated circles are used as symbols and scaled so that their areas are in a linear proportion with the real-world magnitudes they represent, then the "message" conveyed is incorrect. Numerous other discrepancies between the cartographer's intent and the actual result due to map symbolism have been documented, primarily in the area of magnitude scaling.

There has been no definitive investigation of the extent of this "error term," but numerous studies have all shown that it is quite large. These have ranged from general research on the nature of the problem, such as Jenks's 1970 review of the extent of the error in thematic mapping, to the more numerous investigations of specific components of the cartographic assembly. The latter include, for example, studies in typographic legibility (Bartz 1969, 1970); the reading of statistical symbols (Flannery 1971), the judgment of line weight (R. D. Wright 1967) or of color symbolism (Cuff 1972, 1973). No attempt will here be made to apportion responsibility among the cartographer, the map percipient, or any outside factors for the portions of M and U falling in S_e. The problem of the strategy to be employed to minimize the error quantities in the cartographic communication system is a matter of prime concern in cartography (Robinson 1971; Muehrcke 1972). Among other things it may well involve the construct of an "average map percipient" similar in concept to a kind of humanized economic man (Robinson 1970).

The final matter yet to be treated in this survey of the cartographic communication system is the problem of measuring the quantity of geographical data encoded and transmitted by a map. Such a concept can encompass quite a range, from the simple notion of "there is more on this map than on that one" to measures of the "complexity" of a map, which presumably would be useful in studying questions of comparative map generalization and map design (Muehrcke 1973). The problem of the quantitative assessment of map content has come under review only in recent years and promises to be a difficult one. Because it involves the measurement of the information provided by a map, a seemingly reasonable possibility would be that a solution to the problem might be found in the methods of information theory. On the contrary, it is the authors' conviction that, although something conceptually similar to the techniques of information theory may well have some limited use in special cartographic analyses, the fundamental concepts upon which information theory rests make its direct application in cartographic communication impossible.

Information theory had its beginnings in the late 1920s at the Bell Laboratories when Hartley (1928), an electrical engineer, developed a mathematical formulation for the capacity of various systems of telecommunications to transmit electronic signals representing verbal language. These basic ideas were extended by Wiener (1948) and by Shannon and Weaver (1949) culminating in laws having to do with matching the coding of messages to the noise characteristics of the channel. As Weaver clearly observed, the word "information" in information theory is used in a special sense not to be confused with meaning; two messages, one meaningful and one nonsense, can be equivalent in terms of their information content (Shannon and Weaver 1949). The message of information in information theory is based upon the principle of uncertainty in the sense that a greater number of possible choices indicates more uncertainty, and the greater the uncertainty the greater the information capacity simply because more choices are available. The unit of uncertainty, i.e., information, is based upon the two equally likely choices in a binary system and is called the *bit*, a contraction of "binary unit." Logarithms to the base 2 are employed to express the amount of information, so that the measure of the information content of a simple binary system would be unity, i.e., $\log_2 2 = 1$. All elements of a coding system are not necessarily equally probable, however, so that the measure is determined by summing the products of the logarithms of the probability, p, of every element each multiplied by that same probability, as in

$$H = -\sum_{i=1}^{n} p_i \log_2 p_i$$

This summation is designated by H and called entropy, because of .ts analogy to the quality of random disorganization called entropy in statistical mechanics. Since the maximum value of H for a system would be attained when all its elements are equally probable (Singh 1966, pp. 15–21), H is therefore a simple measure of uncertainty, and the greater the freedom of choice (uncertainty), the more the information. It is apparent, then, that meaning, in the ordinary sense, and information in information theory are essentially the inverse of one another. This has been recognized by Bertin:

> ... if "information" is the improbable [uncertain], maximum information is maximum improbability, that is, total spontaneity. But meaningful perception is a relationship (Fechner); and the relationship between two complete spontaneities, that is, between two completely unknown things, has no meaning. (personal communication, in French, 4 Jan. 1972)

It is surprising that this "essential paradox," as Bertin calls it, has not received more attention from those interested in applying the techniques of information theory in contexts other than electronic communication.

The lure of information theory as a possible method for quantifying the content of various communication systems has been great, partly because of its tremendous impact on the understanding of the processes connected with the transmission of signals (Bar-Hillel

1964, p. 283). Psychology was immediately attracted to the apparent potential of information theory, especially in the area of perception. Numerous papers and books appeared, but by the 1960s doubts about its direct applicability were being voiced. For example, Pierce remarked:

> It seems to me, however, that while information theory provides a central, universal structure and organization for electrical communication it constitutes only an attractive area in psychology. It also adds a few new and sparkling expressions to the vocabulary of workers in other areas. [1961, p. 249]

One field of research in psychology, analogically close to map perception, is figure perception. The inability of information theory to contribute much in this area is spelled out in detail by Green and Courtis (1966); the expressive title of their paper is "Information Theory and Figure Perception: The Metaphor that Failed." They point out (p. 12) that for information theory to be employed in any perceptual investigation, among the requirements that have to be met are: (1) an agreed-upon alphabet of signs with known and constant probabilities of occurrence, and (2) objectivity of the probabilities. Green and Courtis demonstrate clearly that in the perception of two-dimensional graphic arrays of marks, neither requirement can be met when one attempts to measure the "information content," even though the requirements are "readily justified in the original context in which information theory was developed ... " (p. 13). They go on to emphasize that information theory is concerned with components (and the probabilities of their occurrence) which are to be perceived in linear sequences, and, as we shall see in a subsequent chapter, this is totally different from the perception of a two-dimensional array of marks in a figure (map).

The assumption of linearity in information theory—that is, the sequential pattern in telecommunication systems—is clearly stated even in Hartley's pioneering paper of 1928:

> In any given communication the sender ... selects a particular symbol and ... causes the attention of the receiver to be directed to that particular symbol. By successive selections a sequence of symbols is brought to the listener's attention. [p. 536]

As will be discussed in detail in a subsequent chapter, we do not perceive the elements of two- (or three-) dimensional displays in any strict sequence, but in the unified and interrelated form of a

Gestalt. To be sure, there will be some sequential pattern of eye movement involved in the total view, but research on eye movements so far indicates that the patterns are relatively varied and unpredictable (Jenks 1973). Green and Courtis (1966) point out (p. 31) that one can impose a linear sequence on the perception of a figure, but that this completely distorts the normal situation, since "Perception of a sequence of relationships between points [or signals] is a very different process from that of the perception of simultaneous relationships between parts [of a figure]." Also, they note that one can break up a figure (abstract picture, design, map, etc.) into cells for a summary analysis, unit by unit, but they note that "this is not how it is *seen* by the percipient."

Another very significant element in the problem, which we will later discuss in detail, is that the amount of knowledge conveyed by a map (figure) is not only a function of the cartographer but of the percipient as well. Furthermore, even with respect to language, Green and Courtis (1966) make the very important point that

> the alphabet of signs is not one of letters or words, but of meaning units, which are ... peculiar to the individual. What is transmitted may be regarded by an engineer as simple, a string of words, or letters and spaces for that matter, but what is *communicated* is a set of meanings ... the essential property of language is not to be found in Markov chains but in syntactic constituents ... which leaves information theory right back where it started—a mathematical tool in communication engineering, particularly useful for dealing with the technical problems of channel capacity. [pp. 32–33]

Another parallel between figural perception and map perception is that of blank spaces. In a caricature drawing what is left out, so to speak, is often very meaningful because of the input of the percipient. Green and Courtis refer to this in a very perceptive section analyzing cartoon drawings (pp. 20–27). In cartography, a blank space can contain a great deal of information by experienced inference, such for example as the "empty" area shown between a meandering stream and its (floodplain!) edge shown by the sharp rise of the valley wall. Yet by being blank and homogeneous that area would have to be assessed in information theory as containing zero bits of information.

The possibility of measuring the information content of a map, and by subtraction assessing the efficiency of its transmission, lured cartographers to attempt to apply the techniques of information theory in mapping. For example, Roberts reported that a standard U.S.G.S. quadrangle contains between a hundred and two hundred million bits of information, and a variety of other assessments and applications have been made (e.g., Hake 1970; Sukhov 1970; Gokhman, Meckler, and Polizhayev 1970; and Balasubramanyan 1971). Sukhov's study illustrates the basic problems referred to above. In an analysis of a map made by superimposing a grid of cells, he determined the "information content" to be 1,025.1 bits per cm^2. Disregarding the problem of equating the "information content" of one symbol as opposed to another, the practice of summing the "information content" in the cells of an arbitrary grid totally disregards the positional factor. In other words, if the cells were rearranged so that the resulting array was absolute geographical nonsense, the "information content" would still be the same. Furthermore, the probabilities must be assigned in some quite arbitrary way, for there is no simple geographical equivalent to such things as word and letter frequency or linguistic redundancy.

Because the communication of the "information" on a map is in no way like that of a coded sequential message consisting of signals, the measurement of the "information content" of a map and of the amount transmitted by a cartographer to a map percipient cannot be effectively obtained with the techniques of information theory. We will have to search for other ways to assess M_3 in Fig. 2.8.

Although the direct application of information theory seems not to provide a method for assessing the actual "information content" of a map, some analytical method similar in concept may be useful in quantifying some of the characteristics of a map of concern to the cartographer. For example Muehrcke, in a summary of approaches to analyzing "pattern complexity" in maps (1973), suggests the utilization of the general concept of redundancy as a measure of this attribute of a map. Because he retains a fixed "alphabet" by limiting the application to a specific class of maps, and because the "alphabet" varies along only one dimension (numbers of class intervals), the application is legitimate. Even though the redundancy sums themselves may not have any absolute validity in the sense that they do not actually assess the total "information content," the general approach of information theory can provide a useful basis for comparison (Salichtchev and Berliant 1973, pp. 162–63). It seems reasonable that a quantity similar to that of entropy (H), arrived at by some as yet undevised method, may be developed to quantify such attributes as "systematic regularity"—or its opposite "visual disorganization"—"figural dominance," and other such qualities not now well understood and subsumed by the term "pattern complexity." Presumably, such attributes should be related to the quantity of information communicated by a map. What is needed, however, is not simply the direct application in cartography of the mathematical–statistical techniques of another field, but the development of techniques, perhaps through adaptation, to the unique conditions of cartography (Kádár, Ágfalvi, Lakos, and Karsay 1973; Molineux 1974).

In this chapter we have seen that mapping is basically an attempt at communication between the cartographer and the map percipient. Although there may be fundamental differences between the kinds of "messages" being conveyed by various classes of maps, all maps have as their aim the transfer of images of the geographical milieu. Analyses by cartographers of the communication process have tended to concentrate on the flows and summary character of the operations involved in the communication, primarily as a means of identifying the components and interrelationships among the various operations which make up the field of cartography. It seems entirely possible to identify the basic components of the field of cartography in a "macro-sense" by surveying its activities, as they have been described briefly in this chapter. On the other hand, any thorough understanding of the field depends upon a greater penetration in which man's perceptual and cognitive processes are probed. We shall begin this in the next chapter, which will deal with mapping as a fundamental subset of graphic communication and with its cognitive essentials.

3 Mapping, Language, and Meaning

In the museum I learned the bitter way how inadequate words are as tools for description, definition, and classification of objects each of which is unique.

W. M. Ivins, Jr.

The proverb, presumably Chinese, which asserts that "one picture is worth a thousand words" has often been put forward by cartographers in support of the virtues of the map as a form of communication. It is quite likely that its originator, as well as all those who have since repeated it, believed that the advantage of the picture was primarily one of economy: although it might take a thousand words to convey a given meaning, one could do it by either one picture or a multiplicity of words. Generally speaking, this is not true.

The map (picture) is a singular form of communication, and it has few of the characteristics of what we call "language," namely, meaningful patterns of vocal sounds, and their corresponding written symbols. The two systems, map and language, are essentially incompatible (Petchenik 1974, p. 66). To be sure, we use the term "language" loosely to denote any method of communication; but to believe that the language systems of maps and words are somehow equivalent and therefore convertible is as wrong as asserting that the "language" of algebra could be used to communicate the meaning of a Rembrandt. The nonconformity of mapping with the language of words also suggests that there may well be insurmountable obstacles to the employment in cartographic theory of such word-language concepts as grammar and syntax.

In this chapter we shall examine the distinction between maps and verbal language with the hope that by contrasting these basically different methods of communication we can demonstrate and clarify the exceptional nature of mapping. We shall conclude with a consideration of what elements of knowledge are unique to this system, that is, what is the essential meaning involved in mapping.

Ivins's remark, quoted at the head of this chapter (1953, p. 51), about the nature of objects in a museum and the difficulty of using words to communicate about unique objects, has as much relevance for the cartographer or geographer as it has for the museum curator.

43

The ultimate object or complex about which the cartographer is concerned to communicate is the milieu, as previously defined, the ultimate phenomenon being the unique arrangement of things therein. The general nature of words that makes them so useful and adaptable for description, definition, and classification, is not at all well suited for communication of such a unique spatial complex. Hence, although other forms of communication and knowledge can in some respects be compared to maps, as was observed in the first chapter, the unique aspects of maps and mapping tend to be either overlooked or intentionally ignored.

In comparing the nature of mapping with the character of ordinary verbalizing, we are confronted immediately with a difficulty that is symptomatic and revealing. As suggested above, in casual use the term "language" can refer, loosely, to the way in which human beings communicate anything, from thought conveyed by complex assemblages of words or mathematical symbols to emotions conveyed by gestures. In this general sense mapping, too, can be considered a language, for it allows communication about the milieu among those who understand the rules and characteristics of mapping. But when used more precisely the term "language" refers to the exchange of thought among humans by means of a culture-specific set of sounds and images, consisting of spoken and written letters, words, and a structural grammar. The difficulty is that whereas all aspects of verbal language, including its structure and application whether in speaking, writing, or reading are subsumed by the term "language," as we noted earlier there is no such general and comparable term for the analogues of these aspects in the communication of spatial knowledge in maps and mapping. Consequently, we have had to define existing words in constricted ways for purpose of analysis. "Mapping," although normally a participle, will be used here as a gerund to denote the entire system with its own structure and processes, including the concepts of mapper and percipient, as defined in Chapter 1.

When used with respect to verbal language, the term "reading" refers to the process by which someone familiar with a particular language in its spoken and written forms can apprehend meaning from a series of figures (letters) representing sounds that encode the meaning intended by their author. The reader apprehends the intended meaning by poorly understood, complex processes of eye-brain interaction. By carrying out a linear sequence of eye fixations on a series of figures, the reader is able to reconstruct a sequence of thought generated by someone other than himself. In contrast, the meaning of a map is contained in a figure, consisting of a complex array of potential sub-figures viewed in a nonlinear, unpredictable series of visual fixations (Jenks 1973). (It is necessary to qualify the sub-figures as "potential" because figural quality appears to be a characteristic arising in part from the apprehender, not simply from the graphic array itself.) It is almost as if one had to read from a page where all the words had been assembled in random order: obviously there could be no fixed starting point or sequence of perception. Moreover, the word "reading" is not used in connection with verbal language to refer to anything less complete than the apprehension of meaning; that is, if someone views and describes the shapes of the letter-images on a page of text written in a language not known to him, this process would not be called "reading." In connection with map use, however, this distinction is not at all clear. Anyone who looks at a map and sees something, perhaps red lines, would ordinarily be referred to as a "map reader," even though the red lines might mean absolutely nothing to him. Hence, the distinction between simply viewing a meaningless graphic array and perceiving a meaningful figure is basic, and we must use different terms to preserve this distinction. We shall call the person who merely sees the red lines a "map viewer" in contrast to the percipient, as defined in Chapter 1, who is a mapper who sees a meaningful figure.

The cartographer intends to communicate some knowledge of the arrangement of things in real space by using a system of arraying graphic marks on a smaller, representative space (paper, or whatever surface is used). As is true of the reader of text, the map percipient understands some of the intended information on the basis of a complex interaction of eye and brain. But certain differences between the text reader and the map percipient are fundamental: the text reader must follow a particular sequence in his acts of visual perception, and he must relate his visual stimuli to a system of sounds and meanings rather than to another system of visual images. If one merely "looks" at an array of letter-figures, the process is never called "reading." The map percipient, in contrast, can and does enter the graphic array at any point; he can stop at any point; and often he relates the visual stimuli to other visual stimuli, rather than to a system of sounds.

Having compared in a cursory fashion the disparate processes of acquiring meaning from text and from maps, we can now turn to a more systematic consideration of the relation between verbalizing and mapping—that is, between the structure of verbal communication, for which we use the general term "language," and the structure of mapping-communication, for which there is, unfortunately, no such broad term. At the outset we must note that the philosophical literature concerned with the relation between images and knowledge, or images and words, tends to be somewhat confusing. Even the word "image" can have quite different meanings. We concern ourselves here with two: one kind of image is the external physical array of materials that produces perceptible contrasts and recognizable shapes, such as an actual object or a picture of it; while the other image is an internal phenomenon, where the internal counterpart of something like an external image is generated. That is, a person is said to have an "image" of something when he *reacts* as though he were actually looking at a physical image, when in fact he is not. The external image is a relatively simple thing to characterize and describe, while the internal image must ultimately be a construct of memory, belief, or inference, rather than immediate direct observation. These two meanings of the term "image" are interwoven throughout the remainder of this essay, but the context will make the distinction clear.

Some have argued that all knowledge is ultimately rooted in images, while others make a distinction between the roles of words and images. Blanshard argues clearly that thinking and imagery are two entirely different things, related but not directly comparable. He notes that imagery is useful as a support to thinking, that it has unique values of its own, but that it is not the same as thinking:

> Even though imaging cannot be generally identified with thinking, it does provide an important support to it. Imagery supports thinking much as words do, and much as sensation supports perceiving. Thought sets out in the beginning from the shore of immediacy, and is reluctant to lose its anchorage there. In the firmness and vividness of sensation, in the definite movements of the spoken word, in the image, whose sensible quality is so like that of the actual thing, there is something secure to tie to. . . . But if thought can be linked to imagery, the fugitive and elusive ideas gain by contact something of the stability of the image. Thus in most thinking the work of the image is the same as the work of words. The image is not the idea, yet it is far too useful an aid to be thrown away. [1948, 1:554]

Arguments such as Blanshard's concerning the relationship between words and images have long fallen within the domain of philosophers, but they are now becoming a legitimate subject for increasing attention from experimental psychologists. It appears that many long-standing issues in this area will be resolved through the innovative research techniques and analytical structures of the kind contained in *Visual Information Processing* (1973). Cooper and Shepard, contributors to that volume, describe the approaches now being taken in psychology:

> Following a long period of behaviorist-induced skepticism regarding the possibility of a scientific study of mental events, increasing experimental and theoretical effort is now being directed toward an understanding of the internal states and processes by means of which we represent objects and events in the external world. . . . In particular, much of the recent research on mental images and mental transformations with which we shall be concerned here can be viewed as a search for experimental paradigms that yield behaviorial evidence to confirm and to elaborate the models for mental processes that are suggested by introspection. [1973, p. 75]

An appreciation of the general character and value of images is basic to any understanding of maps, since the map constitutes a particular case of the general class of *image*. Although most cartographers assume that maps have unique values, the nature of these has not often been stressed or developed. The written word is also an image, but consideration of words as figures-on-ground is an aspect of language that provides no particular insight into the comparison of language and mapping. The triviality of considering words as images (except, of course, in a specific study of that topic, such as in a psychological study of word perception) is so firmly established that most authors, in comparing words and images, put them at opposite ends of a continuum.

Throughout his book, Ivins (1953) is concerned with contrasting the basically different forms of communication represented by words and pictures. Although he is interested in the specific nature of pictures, there is much that maps and pictures have in common, and his statements about the nature of pictures seem thoroughly applicable to maps. Ivins points out that all knowing and thinking can be communicated from one person to another only if they are given a physical form, i.e., symbols: "Of the various methods of making such symbolic communication, there can be little doubt that the two most useful and important are provided by words and pictures" (p. 158). He explains the fundamental differences between the two forms in simple terms:

> While both words and pictures are symbols, they are different in many ways of the greatest importance. So little are they equivalent to each other that if communication were confined to either alone, it would become very limited in its scope. All words need definitions, in the sense that to talk about things we have to have names for them. Verbal definition is a regress from word to word, until finally it becomes necessary to point to something which we say is what the last word in the verbal chain of definition means. Frequently the most convenient way of pointing is to make a picture. [pp. 158–59]

In the same way that a picture replaces the act of pointing to something, the map serves (in one of its aspects) to point to the milieu. Furthermore, picture symbols are far more specific than word symbols. For example, the *word* "chair" is a term with a general meaning quite distinct from specific details of style, color, and so on, but on the other hand, any *picture* of "chair" must refer to a particular chair. This specificity makes the picture either more or less useful, depending on the need one has for "chair information." Similarly, a map provides information about particular places, or provides specific images; in this sense it has both unique value and distinct limitations as a medium for communication.

One of the analyses of the relation between language and image that appears most useful to cartography has been developed by Langer (1951), who makes apparent the futility of equating the structure of mapping with that of verbal language. Her analysis of the relation of symbolic activity in general to the specific aspects of image development is important for an understanding of mapping. The "new key," which is the central theme of Langer's book, begins where empiricism (long the favored approach in science and philosophy) leaves off:

> The problem of observation is all but eclipsed by the problem of *meaning*. And the triumph of empiricism in science is jeopardized by the surprising truth that our *sense-data are primarily symbols*. Here, suddenly it becomes apparent that the age of science has begotten a new philosophical issue, inestimably more profound than its original empiricism: for in all quietness,

along purely rational lines, mathematics has developed just as brilliantly and vitally as any experimental technique, and step by step, has kept abreast of discovery and observation; and all at once, the edifice of human knowledge stands before us, not as a vast collection of sense reports, but as a structure of *facts that are symbols and laws that are their meanings.* A new philosophical theme has been set forth. . . . The power of symbols is its cue, as the finality of sense-data was the cue of a former epoch. [p. 29]

Symbols are seen not only as organizers of belief and of knowledge, but are the means through which belief and knowledge are attained. Blanshard (1948) makes a similar point: " 'sense data', instead of being hard little pellets offered us by nature, are so plastic to thought that to catch them in an untouched state is really a vain attempt." (1:20). Langer shares the belief, with many others, that "this basic need, which certainly is obvious only in man, is the *need of of symbolization.* The symbol-making function is one of man's primary activities, like eating, looking or moving about. It is the fundamental process of his mind, and goes on all the time" (p. 45). She finds speech to be the readiest active termination of this basic process in the human brain, the symbolic transformation of experience. Its communicative value, she finds, comes only at a later stage. Piaget, too, has noted how young children speak at great length with no particular intent of communication, and with no interest in the response of others to what they say.

The transformation of "facts" or experience into symbols is accomplished by a system of projection, the form of which may not be realized and which may result in deceptive symbols. Langer, in fact, resorts to mapping for an analogy to clarify the nature and consequence of this projection process:

"Projection" is a good word, albeit a figurative one, for the process by which we draw *logical* analogies. Geometric projection is the best instance of a perfectly faithful representation which, without knowledge of some logical rule, appears to be a misrepresentation. A child looking at a map of the world in Mercator projection cannot help believing that Greenland is larger than Australia: he simply *finds* it larger. The projection employed is not the usual principle of copying which we use in all visual comparison or translations, and his training in the usual rule makes him unable to "see" by the new one. . . .

> Language . . . contains a law of projection of which
> philosophers are sometimes unaware, so that their reading of
> the presented "facts" is obvious and yet wrong, as a child's
> visual experience is obvious yet deceptive when his judgment is
> ensnared by the trick of the flattened map. The transformation
> which facts undergo when they are rendered as propositions is
> that the relations in them are turned into something like
> *objects.* [1951, pp. 75–76]

Furthermore, the projection process involved in language includes a system which requires that names and named relations or activities be strung out side by side, in an order that may or may not have anything to do with the spatial or temporal order of the topic, concepts or other things discussed. Langer calls this property of verbal symbolism "discursiveness," and "by reason of it, only thoughts which can be arranged in this peculiar order can be spoken at all; any idea which does not lend itself to this 'projection' is ineffable, incommunicable by means of words" (p. 77).

For experiences that defy linguistic projection, such as those in space, nondiscursive forms of symbolism have developed. Their primary function is the conceptualization of the assemblage of lines, colors, tones, and forms, to provide apprehendable images in place of a confusion of sensations. Langer finds that such visual forms are just as capable of articulation, of coherent combination, as are the words of a language, but recognizes that "the laws that govern this sort of articulation are altogether different from the laws of syntax that govern language. The most radical difference is that *visual forms are not discursive.* They do not present their constituents successively, but simultaneously" (p. 86). There are many differences between presentational symbolism (mapping) and discursive symbolism. Langer observes that

> Language in the strict sense is essentially discursive; it has
> permanent units of meaning which are combinable into larger
> units; it has fixed equivalences that make definition and
> translation possible, its connotations are general, so that it
> requires non-verbal acts, like pointing, looking, or emphatic
> voice-inflections, to assign specific meaning to its terms. [p. 89]

In contrast, presentational symbolism is not discursive, cannot be translated, does not allow of definitions within its own system, and cannot directly convey generalities. Langer states clearly that in contrast to discourse

> the meanings of all other symbolic elements that compose a
> larger, articulate symbol [such as a map] are understood only
> though the meaning of the whole, through their relations within
> the total structure. Their very functioning as symbols depends
> on the fact that they are involved in a simultaneous, integral
> presentation. [p. 89]

The fundamental difference between discursive and presentational symbolism is well illustrated by a simple black-and-white
photograph. As Langer points out (1951, p. 88), whereas the various
elements of a language, words, have fixed meanings and can be
combined into composite symbols with new meanings, sentences,
paragraphs, etc. (according to the rules established for the language), the elements of light and dark that make up a photograph by
themselves have no significance whatever. They are simply parts
reflecting more or less light. Yet *taken together,* these elements
constitute a faithful representation of the graphic character of the
visual object. Ordinarily there are a great many more visual
components than there are commonly available verbal elements to
describe the parts of the picture—there is not just one single part
corresponding to a "mouth" in a portrait; instead, it is made up of
many shapes and tones. Because of the continuous nature of these
visual elements it is impossible to isolate the smallest independent
symbol, and recognize its identity when it is encountered in some
other contexts. Langer concludes:

> Photography, therefore, *has no vocabulary.* The same is
> obviously true of painting, drawing, etc. There is, of course, a
> technique of picturing objects, but the law governing this
> technique cannot properly be called a "syntax" since there are
> no items that might be called, metaphorically, the "words" of
> portraiture. [p. 88]

Since there are no "words," there can be no lexicon of meanings for
lines, hues, tones, and the other elements of pictorial technique.
Ivins makes a similar point, with some variation. He agrees that
there are no dictionary definitions for the "lines and spots" of a
picture, and continues:

> It is much as though [in pictures] we had dictionary defini-
> tions for sentences and paragraphs but not for individual
> words. . . . With rare exceptions, we see a picture first as a
> whole, and only after having seen it as a whole do we analyze it

into its component parts. We can begin this analysis at any place in the picture and proceed in any direction, and the final result is the same in every case. [p. 61]

When we analyze maps as a form of symbolism we find that they do not fit clearly into the categories of either discursive or presentational symbolism, although certainly maps are fundamentally much more nearly presentational than discursive. Clearly, as in a picture, the elements of a map do take their ultimate meaning from the whole: they may change meaning with context, since there is no syntax that is retained from one presentation to another. "Syntax" is perhaps the most thoughtlessly used word one encounters in writing where an attempt is made to compare maps with verbal language. With respect to language it refers to the temporal relations of words as they are spoken (or linear as they are written), where the sequence of emission and apprehension is prescribed and fixed. On maps, there exists no such temporal order, and an analogy with spatial arrangement has no meaning, since this is uniquely prescribed by the area mapped. There is no predictable sequence of element presentation or apprehension, comparable to language, and no element has meaning apart from the whole.

Maps are far more stylized than most pictorial representations. Unlike the photograph, where the elements of light and dark cannot be said to correspond exactly to the verbalized elements of the object pictured, most ordinary maps are made to retain a systematic correspondence of the graphic element with the verbal category of element represented; for example a homogeneous red line may stand for a particular kind of road, wherever such a road appears on the map. Unlike pictures, maps usually have legends that serve to translate from verbal presentation to graphic presentation or vice versa; moreover, representation techniques are carried from one map to another far more often than is the case in other forms of presentational symbolism. Furthermore, maps ordinarily present an image of the same object, the earth milieu, and this then is the ultimate "unique" object, for which Ivins found words inadequate in the quotation at the head of this chapter. Maps present different portions of the earth and different aspects of those portions; but when one looks at an image that has been assigned the label "map," one expects that the image will have as its counterpart in meaning a portion of or all the earth as an object with a complex surface. The particular graphic techniques utilized on the map indicate which unique area is being shown, and what characteristics of it are presented in that particular map.

Insofar as the content of the symbolic presentation is concerned, it is difficult to define a map. All presentational symbolism is concerned with the depiction of spatial relations, that is, with the logic of part-whole relations. But aside from the fact that ordinarily maps are of the earth (or something celestial) the attribute that seems to set maps apart is the way in which they represent reality with respect to a particular scale of spatial relations. Cartographers are not concerned with mapping at all scales of spatial relation. The arrangement of the components of a molecule of DNA, for example, may obviously be "mapped"; this molecule occupies space on the earth, and such a mapping activity might seem to be a logical counterpart of the mapping of the arrangement of streets within a city. In common usage, however, such sub-microscopic mapping lies outside the activity of the cartographer, as do the scales of architectural and engineering drawing. Of course, there is nothing absolute that prescribes limits; it is strictly a matter of utility based on relationship to the size of a human being. Blanshard comments: Our practical dealings, and therefore our perceptions, move in the intermediate range, among things that bear manageable proportion to our own bodies; if our bodies were the size of an ant's, tables and mountains could hardly figure" (1948, 1:132).

Mapping also differs from some other forms of presentational symbolism in that it often depicts a view that has not actually been seen, a fact that is overlooked in many analyses of the nature of mapping. We tend to think of a map as a bird's-eye view, or more recently as an astronaut's view, but such an analogy is misleading. Maps are a construction, an abstraction, an arrangement of markings that relates to spatial "reality" only by agreement, not by sensory testability. Quite apart from the mathematical transformation required in mapping, maps have an underlying "projection" system that is similar to what Langer describes for all language. One may traverse the area covered by a large-scale topographic map and find a point-by-point agreement between the perceptual reality and the mapped information. This is not analogous to the sequence of words in discursive language, for one could move in any direction. In any case, one would not have "seen" the area whole, that is, experienced all the depicted relations simultaneously, as one does when confronted with the map-image of the same space. In this respect the map not only provides point information, but it provides the non-flier with an image of a "whole."

Clearly, mapping is a form of presentational symbolism, but it must be recognized that maps do not fit the category without considerable qualification. The map surface usually contains letters and words that would at first appear to relate it to written discourse. But, insofar as the words on maps are unique names, not class symbols, they serve in the same "point-to" capacity as does a picture. In fact, each non-class name converts a class symbol—for example, a city dot—to a unique object or phenomenon; thus, in function, the names are more nearly like pictures than like written discourse.

Sometimes the logical structure of a complex phenomenon can be comprehended by determining what one must learn. about the phenomenon in order to use it. For example, in attempting to understand the nature of verbal language, it has been profitable to conduct research into the manner in which infants learn the vocabulary and rules which constitute the grammar of the language of their culture. Looking at maps in a similar way, we can ask: "What is it that must be known before someone can change from being merely a map viewer to being a map percipient?" We can extend our mapping–language comparison with this approach.

Using some of the vocabulary developed by Langer, it appears that in learning discursive symbolism—language—three major aspects must be assimilated: projective technique, words, and syntax. The first term has to do with the way one learns to transform raw sensory impressions into language, and to the kinds of situations that permit the application of discourse. Words, of course, represent objects and actions. Syntax refers to the rules having to do with word sequence within the structure of a particular language. When a child is born into a culture, he takes his place in a situation in which the grammatical characteristics of discourse have been firmly established. Projective techniques are not taught in any explicit way, but words and syntax are learned both informally and through schooling. Learning mapping can be analyzed in a similar fashion, but there are more dissimilarities than similarities.

In the map parallel to the language aspect of projective technique, the most important problems concern what constitutes the appropriate domain of mapping as a particular form of presentational symbolism, and how continuous sensory information is quantized and transformed for the purpose of this domain. In this regard, it is readily recognized that all maps are concerned to depict the idea "where." Man has always been concerned with the spatial relationships of tangible objects and the phenomenological variation that is apparent as one moves about the earth's surface. The essential meaning of maps can be stated, then, as "consequential spatial arrangement," and such arrangement is what is "projectable" to the presentational symbolism of mapping. Other less tangible characteristics of objects or relations in space are projectable as well, as for example when the quality or quantity of a mapped referent is depicted; but sheer relative location is the informational domain best handled symbolically by mapping.

The ubiquitousness of spatial considerations in human intellectual development has been noted by Cassirer and other philosophers and was underscored in Chapter 1. "Arranging" seems to be a fundamental human activity, and man's most basic form of arranging deals with objects in real space. From this elemental activity, human intellectual development has proceeded to the notion of a representational space in which objects can be transformed at will, and from there to the arranging of concepts and objects in a conceptual space. The opening sentence in a statistics book puts it simply: "Data may be viewed as relations between points in a space" (Coombs 1964, p. 1).

It is clear that the arrangement of things in space can be represented in ways other than by mapping. Although words and even equations can be used to tell where something is in relation to something else, these representational tools are little used in this domain because they lack the quality of *image*, the most comprehensible form in which spatial arrangement can be encoded or transmitted. The potential for image development is the most elegant attribute of the map. As Blanshard has noted, the image is probably prior to and more basic than words and thought; it is invaluable in the activity of arrangement. We can summarize, then, by saying that the primary aspect of mapping that must be learned is the domain of spatial reality for which such imagery is the most efficient form of symbolism.

Words are the second aspect of discursive language that the child must learn, but for this there is no analogue in mapping. As we have seen earlier in this essay, there is no corresponding unit in presentational symbolism. The act of learning a word requires fixing the association of a sound or sequence of sounds with an object or process. Learning to read adds the need to equate images (letters) with sounds, and to acquire meaning from them as one would from the sounds. Clearly, there are no strictly comparable visual units that are carriers of fixed meanings in presentational symbolism, and thus in mapping. By disregarding this fundamental point, a number of analyses of maps from a "linguistic" point of view have foundered, and must continue to fail.

Finally, as has been noted earlier, there is essentially no counterpart in mapping to the syntax of discursive language. The arrangement of words in a particular order for the purpose of conveying specific meanings—"man hits car," for example, in contrast with "car hits man"—has at most only a very limited parallel in static mapping, and even then not in the basic fashion that one deals linguistically with the order of the fundamental building blocks: words. In mapping, the "order" of the elemental units of meaning is prescribed by their arrangement in space. To be sure, one can manipulate the positioning of elements to some extent by varying the system of (mathematical) projection or by making map distance correspond to other kinds of "distance," such as travel time, cost, or mental distance, rather than measured earth distance. But these are hardly comparable to the syntax of language. Animated maps, like other motion pictures, appear in a time sequence and thus can have a kind of syntactical structure (Wendt 1962; Cornwell and Robinson 1966), but that has nothing to do with the map per se. The development of hierarchial levels, as in a graphic outline (Robinson and Sale 1969, pp. 266–69), is another kind of ordering, but only vaguely approximates the concept of syntax.

It should be abundantly clear by now that about the only real correspondence between language, as discursive symbolism, and mapping, as presentational symbolism, is that they are both methods of communication; and there the similarity stops. Nevertheless, the review of the essential characteristics of language has provided a useful means of examining the characteristics of mapping. Missing so far, however, has been any real consideration of what it is in mapping that carries meaning and how this aspect is also fundamentally different from discursive language. For this, too, we shall first turn to language.

Langer develops the idea of "pair-relations" in discussing meaning in language (1951, p. 58). One can focus upon the relation between several kinds of pairs—that between the object and the word, between the user and the word, or between the user and the object named. With variations, the pair-relation concept also proves useful in an analysis of the "unit of meaning" of a map. A map is usually composed of signs on paper, in the form of individual units, such as lines, continuous tones, or flat screens. But the perceptual item is not mere undifferentiated signs, but rather the forms that they create. For the viewer, these forms have shape, extent, hue, value, and so on, and are perceived as unitary graphic elements, such as a red line, a green area, a black star, a blue name. We call such a unitary graphic element a map mark, or just a mark. Unlike other forms of presentational symbolism, such as painting or photography, where there are few, if any, graphic units with discrete verbal equivalents, a map usually does have some of these. Red lines stand for roads, black dots for towns, and so on, and in general, there are discrete graphic elements on every map, matched to verbal elements in a legend.

In considering the logical structure of mapping, any map mark can be analyzed as a part of numerous pair-relations; these pair-relations are a fundamental, but not exclusive, aspect of the structure out of which grows meaning. For example, suppose a mapper portrays the distribution of cotton-growing areas in some region by employing a red dot 0.5 mm in diameter to represent 5,000 hectares of cotton. In the following discussion we call the red dot the mark and the 5,000 hectares of cotton the referent. The relationship between at least four pairs can be examined:

1. Mapper - Referent	(How does that mapper conceive of the referent quantity? Why has he chosen to map it? Why this particular unit of cotton-growing area?)
2. Mapper - Mark	(How does the mapper perceive a red dot of this size and color? Why did he choose it?)
3. Referent - Mark	(Why this particular association between cotton-growing areas and red dots of this size?)
4. Mapper - Referent/Mark	(Why did he pair these items?)

These analyses should then be followed by a further pair-relation analysis in which "mapper" is replaced by "map percipient," the person who views and understands the map.

Although the words of language and the marks used on maps can both be subjected to a "pair-relation" type of analysis, we must recognize the limited similarity between words and marks. The crop dealt with in the example above has the name "cotton" in the English language. Obviously no one who wants to communicate with any other English-speaking person would consider using some other idiosyncratic name for this particular crop. The label for this crop (object) is fixed in our culture, and once it is learned it may be used widely and understood in many contexts. In contrast, there is no generally accepted map mark that means "5,000 hectares of cotton," or even "cotton" in general. Each mapper is free to create new associations between marks and their referents, and this condition makes it clear that, unlike the meanings of words in discourse, the fixed element of meaning (the analogue of "word") is missing from the graphic "language" of mapping.

It should be noted that in the recent history of cartography there have been several attempts to change this. The early International Statistical Congresses and the Geological Congresses of the nineteenth century attempted to legislate meanings for map marks. Similar "standardization," more recent and successful, has been accomplished by the International Civil Aviation Organization. In national surveys and in atlas mapping, there has naturally been a systematization of marks and their meanings. The most ambitious move in this direction has been the establishment by the International Cartographic Association of Commission IV, of which a basic objective is such standardization of marks and meanings for thematic cartography. Except in limited circumstances these attempts seem doomed to failure: the complexity of the problem is overwhelming (Board 1973; Robinson 1973; Arnberger 1974).

Let us consider another aspect of map marks that makes them strikingly different from words; they have location. Each mark occupies a particular place and no other in relation to all other marks on the map surface. Given a particular projection transformation system, the existence of one referent point and its equivalent map mark, all other marks on the map can each have only one possible location. Generalization of meaning for map marks exists only in the legend, where, for example, the red dot is set equal to 5,000 hectares of cotton. When the red dot is on the map, it represents a particular portion of the earth surface. The meaning of a red dot is not exactly equivalent to that of any other red dot, even on one map, since no two aggregates of 5,000 hectares of cotton can be at exactly the same location, and certainly not from one map to another. In other words, a simple pair-relation in real map context *cannot* exist; there must always be the referent and its location as well as the mark and its location.

A concept we can call "transparency" raises another major difference between map marks, on the one hand, and on the other, the sounds (or the corresponding letters) that are the physical forms employed in discourse. The sounds of words in verbal exchange are, in themselves, meaningless quantities of sensory impressions. The same can be said for the written form of the language when it is set in the prescribed and very familiar forms of an alphabet in a typeface that attracts little or no attention to itself. When we read or listen, we are virtually unconscious of the perceptual aspects of the words we see or the sounds we hear. We know the meaning well enough, and can easily recall the approximate meaning of a message in spite of having forgotten the exact words and sequence in which they were uttered or written. We may say, then, that the forms of language are transparent to their meaning. Meaning can remain even when the specific words that conveyed or evoked it are forgotten. For someone who is fluent in more than one language, it is quite possible to read something in a certain language, and when finished, be unable to remember which language had been used. Polanyi describes this experience of language transparency strikingly:

> The most pregnant carriers of meaning are of course the
> words of a language, and it is interesting to recall that when we
> use words in speech or writing we are aware of them only in a
> subsidiary manner. This fact, which is usually described as the
> *transparency* of language, may be illustrated by a homely
> episode from my own experience. My correspondence arrives at
> my breakfast table in various languages, but my son under-
> stands only English. Having just finished reading a letter I may
> wish to pass it on to him, but must check myself and look
> again to see in what language it was written. I am vividly
> aware of the meaning conveyed by the letter, yet know nothing
> whatever of its words. I have attended to them closely but only
> for what they mean and not for what they are as objects. If
> my understanding of the text were halting, or its expressions or
> its spelling faulty, its words would arrest my attention. They
> would become slightly opaque and prevent my thought from pas-
> sing through them unhindered to the things they signify.
> [1964, p. 57]

Map marks (including type that appears on the map) differ radically from words by being highly opaque, that is, attracting considerable attention to themselves, rather than to their referents. At any first encounter with a map we are most conscious of colors, shapes, type density, and linework. Rare indeed would be the person who could be less aware of these aspects of the map display than of the "meanings" they convey about the earth's surface. Very likely, many map viewers can proceed little further than this level toward an apprehension of the map as meaning or knowledge, but the more one becomes a "fluent" map percipient, the more the graphic assemblage becomes transparent.

Learning verbal or written language requires the ability to discriminate within a particular domain of sound or a particular assortment of shapes. Map learning involves visual discriminations of a very much wider variety, for the graphic dimensions within which any particular spatial referent may be coded are nearly infinite. There is no limited "alphabet" of map marks. Furthermore, the graphic form with which the existence of a phenomenon in space is depicted on a map will generally convey one or more attributes of the phenomenon other than its sheer existence, albeit usually in a highly generalized or selective fashion (Keates 1972). In language, such attributes or character are conveyed by additional modifying words, that is, not just "chair," but "red chair" or "large chair." Relationships and attributes are labeled, not pictured or analogized. It would be most uncommon, for instance, except in a highly contrived, rebus-like ideogram, to find the word "chair" set in large red type to indicate a large red chair. Quite a different situation prevails in mapping, where the map mark itself may code or show the character as well as the existence of some phenomenon.

The meaning inherent in mapping differs from that in other forms of discourse in another respect. As we have said, a map not only represents a space, but is itself a space. Consequently it can retain the spatial relations among referents, where proportions rather than absolutes are of fundamental interest. This retention of spatial characteristics on the space of the representational surface recalls Korzybski's (1941) retention of "structure" from the territory to the map. Such structural retention may be seen in the form of predictably proportional areas or retained shapes, angles, or proportions among distances. Even more fundamental, and therefore perhaps less obvious, is the fact that topological properties can be retained in mapping: continuous area can be mapped as continuous, closed shapes as closed, near objects can be near, things inside or outside other things can be shown those ways, next to can be next to, and between can be between. For small areas of the earth, it is not difficult to retain these properties of similarity over much of the map. In mapping much larger areas of a sphere on flat paper, however, we become accustomed to considerable "suspension of disbelief." In the retention of such relations in the milieu, it does not seem particularly appropriate to speak of them, as is often done, as being "symbolized" on the map, when in fact reality is actually shown, albeit to scale.

It is significant to note that in the preceding discussion we have avoided using the word "symbol" or "symbolic" in referring to the graphic map marks or the processes involved in selecting them. We prefer to leave "symbol" as a word with a very general meaning in all communication, namely, the form to which sensory experience is converted by the human cognitive system. In this sense all maps are symbols, and all mapping and verbal discourse become symbolic activities. These words are accurate enough, but not useful for any detailed or, more particularly, for any diagnostic or prescriptive analyses.

The concept of representation and meaning in mapping requires that we distinguish clearly between those marks that are visually completely arbitrary, and those that retain some graphic characteristic that can be visually or conceptually related to the referent. Although this distinction does not provide us with sharply divided categories for analysis, it does allow us to establish a linear continuum or scale, at one end of which we can group marks that are more or less visually imitative of their referents, and at the other end, those that have little or no such visual equivalence. We will call the former end of the scale *mimetic depiction* and the latter *arbitrary depiction*.

The mimetic-to-arbitrary map-mark scale concept can be used in analyzing entire maps or specific elements thereof. For example, in mapping the phenomenon of a "city," there are a great many representational alternatives. The map mark samples shown in Fig. 3.1 indicate the range of alternatives insofar as the qualitative–visual aspects of "city" are concerned. There is, it would seem, a natural tendency to move from mimetic to arbitrary depiction as one moves from larger to smaller scale. The ratio of arbitrary to mimetic marks on maps also increases as a society becomes more sophisticated, because the more mimetic a mark, the less it depends for meaning on an associated label or set of words. Continuing this example, we can show a series of map marks for "city" that move from mimetic to arbitrary with respect to variation in the phenomenon, as in Fig. 3.2. The typeface in which the city name is set also can be used to depict city population gradations, in either mimetic or arbitrary fashion, as in Fig. 3.3. Further, even the positioning of map marks, particularly names, can be considered with respect to the mimetic-arbitrary distinction, as in Fig. 3.4.

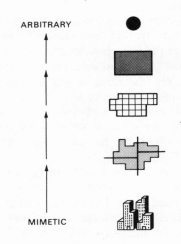

Fig. 3.1. An example of the mimetic to arbitrary range in representation of cities.

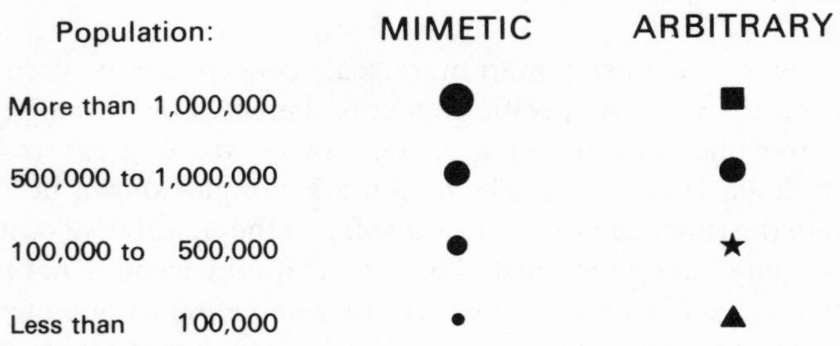

Population:	MIMETIC	ARBITRARY
More than 1,000,000	●	■
500,000 to 1,000,000	●	●
100,000 to 500,000	●	★
Less than 100,000	•	▲

Fig. 3.2. Examples of quantitative variation of marks within the mimetic to arbitrary range.

Population:	MIMETIC	ARBITRARY
More than 1,000,000	Chicago	Chicago
500,000 to 1,000,000	Milwaukee	*Milwaukee*
100,000 to 500,000	Madison	Madison
Less than 100,000	Winnetka	*Winnetka*

Fig. 3.3. Stylistic-quantitative variation in typography within the mimetic to arbitrary range.

Agreement on which map marks are mimetic and which are arbitrary is not likely to be unanimous. It is often assumed that pictorial or semi-pictorial symbols will be correctly interpreted by all viewers because they are "like" the referent; but one viewer's idea of a "factory" may differ significantly from another's. Reactions will vary even more widely when the referent is an aggregate (e.g., "forest") or an abstract concept (e.g., "danger"). A large variety of maps have been produced in recent decades that endeavor to depict the earth surface, the referent, in a "naturalistic fashion." Some of these have been produced by artists and artist-cartographers as "interpretations" of the visible milieu. In ultimate contrast to this approach is the newly developed orthophotomap which covers the map surface with the pattern of marks obtained on the film emulsion of an aerial camera. It is obvious that the "view not seen" aspect of maps enters as a complicating factor. Obviously, no one has experienced the view of the earth surface that the artist-cartographer draws in what he believes to be mimetic fashion, nor have very many persons become accustomed to the perpendicular record of the aerial camera. Rather than being mimetic, both extremes are quite arbitrary. "Realistic" depiction is a relative matter depending on points of view, available visual categories, and especially experience.

There are many different ways in which the marks and the referent might be alike, or thought to be alike. Generally the differentiating characteristic retained in map-mark appearance is that characteristic of the referent considered to be visually prominent and/or graphically distinctive. In addition, there may also be an assumed functional likeness, or even a likeness or equivalence based on common verbal mediation or convention. Examples will make these clearer.

Fig. 3.4. Positioning variation within the mimetic to arbitrary range

Continuous lines on a map frequently represent roads, an obvious "mimetic" situation arising from the fact that roads are continuous, they are linear, they connect two points, and so on. These would be visual and functional likenesses. But there may be conceptual likenesses or analogies as well, and these are more subtle and certainly less consciously attended to in cartography. Suppose that main roads and secondary roads are being shown on the same map. Both, most likely, will be shown as continuous lines. On many maps the main roads might be shown in bright red, cased in black, with the total mark being 1.0 mm wide, while the secondary roads might be a 60 percent screen of black, 0.5 mm wide. There is nothing about the physical characteristics of main roads that would lead one to think of bright red, and most secondary roads are not gray. Main roads, however, are "important" (much used, commonly sought, etc.), and most secondary roads are "unimportant." Therefore, because red tends to be an attention-getting color, and is visually "more important" than gray, the choice of graphic characteristics of the map marks for these two referents reflects a conceptual equating of two different degrees of "importance," matching visual character to utilization character. Even the choice of line width for the two types of roads is likely to have been influenced by this conceptual distinction. Main roads need not be significantly wider than other roads, but conceptually, their represented width has been equated with the experienced degree of their importance.

Even projection characteristics may be regarded from the mimetic-arbitrary point of view. If, for example, in the real-life experience of travel, Town B is closer to Town A than Town C, and if the map projection system retains at least this relationship, it might be regarded as highly mimetic with respect to the arrangement of these points. However, a map can be made with a projection system such that Town C appears closer to Town A. This is legitimate, as long as the projection technique is specified, but it should be considered more "arbitrary." This example of "arbitrary" projection is not quite as clear-cut as the preceding ones, for it is possible that the mapmaker had some likeness in mind that does not match the sensory impressions of most people. He might, for example, have been interested in showing traveling distance among Towns A, B, and C, where map distance from Town A on the map is proportional to travel time from it. Towns A, B, and C might then appear in a different spatial order on the map from that which holds in the real world. This transition has been made from mimetic use of map space (where map distance stands for ground distance, and the units match, e.g., centimeters for kilometers) to arbitrary use (where map distance stands for traveling time, not ground distance, with the use of non-matching units, e.g., centimeters to hours).

The epitome of the arbitrary use of map space is the "cartogram," a particular form of spatial representation which raises interesting conceptual problems whose origins lie in some of the characteristics of mapping we have described. For the most part, mapping in our culture today incorporates an assumption of Euclidean correspondence between the map and the referent territory which is so basic that it is like an article of faith and, consequently, is rarely made explicit (Robinson 1976). This assumption can be stated thus: the map is territory and the referent is territory; therefore spatial relationships on the map are referent spatial relationships, only at a different scale. As we have seen, this correspondence of relationships ordinarily tends to obtain at larger scales, but it is in the nature of the mapping process that it becomes increasingly less valid as the scale becomes smaller because of the difference in the geometric properties of a plane surface (the map) and a spherical surface. It is apparent, to the cartographer at least, that the nature of the projection technique from referent surface to map surface will have an increasingly large effect as one approaches the limiting scale of 1 : infinity, thus leading to different kinds of visual "unreality:" oceans are split, areas are not in correct proportion to one another, the poles become lines rather than points, and so on. Still, map percipients learn to compensate for such "distortion," often intellectually but sometimes, with sufficient experience, even visually. Even in cases of extreme distortion, space still equals space, areas are areas, and so on. In a cartogram, on the other hand, this may not be the case, because the fundamental real-space to real-space relationship between the referent and the map is replaced by an arbitrary utilization of the map surface.

A cartogram may use map space to display something that has very little if any direct relation to space on the referent surface. Such a map may, for example, show numbers of persons, as in a map of the United States, with sizes of state "areas" drawn proportional to the populations of the states. The symbolic sophistication of such a map is of a considerably higher order than it is often considered to be. That portion of the map surface we normally think of as New Jersey in its approximate shape and position to other states is replaced, on an area-stands-for-population cartogram, by a surface that is highly arbitrary when taken alone, but highly mimetic in proportional comparison to the surfaces representing all the other states' populations. That is, letting a quandrangular area of, perhaps, one square centimeter of paper stand for the more than seven million persons who live in New Jersey is totally arbitrary. But, compared to the other surfaces that stand for the populations of other states, there is a somewhat mimetic visual relationship—smaller areas represent smaller numbers of people and larger areas represent larger numbers of people. In such a cartogram, we have, in effect, superimposed a set of surface marks representing total numbers of people associated with state names onto a topologic network or graph, where the nodes are state names, or the geographic area of the state unit compressed to a point. Certain angles, outside-inside relationships, and many proximity relationships may have been retained; but the map space can no longer be regarded as being directly mimetic of earth space. Consequently, the percipient may have considerable difficulty in disregarding a normal pattern of map use that equates real space with real space.

This analysis of mapping as a symbol system has attempted to demonstrate the essential difference between mapping and the system we call language. The differences between the discursive and the presentational forms of communication are so profound and fundamental as to defy any parallelism beyond that of simple sensory impression. Any attempt to apply to mapping the principles of operational structure out of which arise the grammar of a language is wasted effort. On the other hand, as has been demonstrated, the analysis of how the two symbol systems differ greatly clarifies our understanding of mapping. Whereas the intricacies of discursive language have had the benefit of considerable study, the characteristics of presentational communication have had relatively little.

A second objective of this chapter has been to explore the fundamental character of meaning in the mapping system. Mapping is unique in that it inherently expresses the concept of "where" and uses space to represent space. Thus all the complex conceptual aspects of space, topological and geometric, can be dealt with. This is not to imply that mapping is somehow a simpler system than discourse. The analysis of pair relations among referent, mapper, and map mark clearly shows that even in seemingly simple situations the relationships are deceptively complex. The mimetic-arbitrary continuum in the symbology of mapping is also highly complicated and reaches an ultimate when the map space itself is made arbitrary.

The reader will note that in the course of this chapter we have begun to explore the nature of mapping as a form of knowing. The general investigation of this important topic will be advanced still farther in the next chapter. There we shall deal with visual cognition, a subject of obvious importance to an understanding of mapping.

4 Seeing and Mapping

All perceiving is also thinking, all reasoning is also intuition, all observation is also invention.

Rudolph Arnheim

There can be little disagreement with the simple statement that seeing is basic to mapping. But seeing, if it is thought of at all, is too often dismissed simply as a purely physical phenomenon—light rays flowing passively into the eyes and somehow being converted into the shapes and surfaces that make up a visual assembly. Moreover, much of the research conducted in the visual perception of maps is carried on with little recognition or even awareness of the nature of the meaning of that which is viewed, or of the nature of the processes that intervene between sensory input and intellectual product. If, as Neisser points out, visual cognition "deals with the processes by which a perceived, remembered, and thought-about world is brought into being from as unpromising a beginning as the retinal patterns" (1967, p. 4), then some understanding of it is fundamental to cartography. Many of the phenomena and objects commonly put on maps are visible at the earth's surface, and our knowledge of them is naturally affected by the nature of human visual processing. More important, all such phenomena, even those that are invisible in the milieu (e.g., population density), are converted to visual forms on a map, and therefore an understanding of visual cognition is of value in predicting the potential of the map percipient for comprehending the map.

A few basic assumptions underlie much of what follows. In this chapter, seeing will be treated as an active process, a transaction between the individual and the environment, in which the viewer creates some kind of order from the essentially unordered array that is the visual stimulus. We take the position that perception and knowledge are continuous and interact with one another. Blanshard considers sensation to be the nether limit of perception and explicit judgment to be the upper limit, on a type of three-point scale: "But while differing from both of its neighbours, perception has something in common with each. It plainly involves sensation, though

68

sensation moulded and 'interpreted'; it involves judgment, but judgment that is still in the implicit stage" (1948, 1:54). In writing of Piaget's extensive work, Furth stresses that the Swiss psychologist holds a similar point of view: "To divide knowledge into one category based on perception, another one on intelligence is out of the question" (1969, p. 137).

This leads to the second basic assumption, to be elaborated in considerable detail throughout this chapter: There is no constant, apart, "objective" visual reality, either in the milieu or in the map. Rather, there is visual or imaged knowledge constructed and shaped by the viewer on the basis of unordered sensation. There have long been philosophical precedents for the view that man actively organizes his visual input, and we shall consider some of these; now we are beginning to find psychological and neurological evidence that also suggests the validity and utility of this position. We shall consider this in some detail.

Arnheim, in the introduction to his book *Art and Visual Perception*, comments:

> A thoughtful person cannot read these studies [of the psychology of perception] without admiring the active striving for unity and order manifest in the simple act of looking at a simple pattern of lines. Far from being a mechanical recording of sensory elements, vision turned out to be a truly creative grasp of reality—imaginative, inventive, shrewd, and beautiful. [1964, pp. vii–viii]

Bronowski, in writing about the nature of science in general, similarly points up the active, intervening role of human judgment in forming what is too often taken to be "scientific" (and therefore "objective") reality:

> Reality is not an exhibit for man's inspection, labeled "Do not touch." There are no appearances to be photographed, no experiences to be copied, in which we do not take part. Science, like art, is not a copy of nature but a re-creation of her. [1965, p. 20]

Reality may be construed or re-created in any number of forms, and both the sense organs and the intellect may affect the nature of the construction. In such a context, it is difficult to conceive of "objective" sensory experience, for the sense organs themselves are once removed from that which we conceive of as "reality." Langer has been an articulate advocate in philosophical writings of the belief that there is no such thing as pure "seeing:"

> What is directly observable is only a sign of the "physical fact"; it requires interpretation to yield scientific propositions. Not simply seeing is believing, *but seeing and calculating, seeing and translating.* [1951, p. 29]

Langer makes a number of basic points about the nature of the human organism in its ability, even its need, to perform constructive acts of seeing. She argues that the sense organs are not neutral in filtering information from the real world to the brain and points out (p. 85) that ". . . the world of sense is the real world construed by the abstractions which the sense organs immediately furnish." Thinking can take place only with abstractions; it is the nature of the brain and sense organs to produce these, and it is clearly a constructive, not a passive, function. Langer believes that the brain, in fact, is constituted to be an active producer of abstractions or symbols whenever there is any sensory input which it can process, whether or not there is a reason for producing ideas:

> The brain works as naturally as the kidneys and the blood vessels. It is not dormant just because there is no conscious purpose to be served at the moment [in sleep, for instance]. . . . Instead of that, it goes right on manufacturing ideas—streams and deluges of ideas, that the sleeper is not using to *think* with about anything. But the brain is following its own law; it is actively translating experience into symbols, in fulfillment of a basic need to do so. It carries on a constant process of ideation. [1951, p. 46]

One important consequence to mapping of the constant activity of the brain in its interaction with sensory input is that it will attempt to organize anything made available, even that which may be symbolically totally unfamiliar. A visual display cannot go unprocessed. Furthermore, in understanding symbols, the human being shows that he has the power to treat everything about a particular sense-datum as irrelevant, except a certain form that embodies its meaning for a percipient. This form and meaning may be unchanged, even though the symbol may look very different to the eye at different times, because of both its environment and its intrinsic physical nature (shape, etc.). Langer believes the process of abstraction to be a spontaneous one, going on at all times, which involves

> ... a process of recognizing the concept in any configuration
> given to experience, and forming a conception accordingly....
> *Abstractive seeing* is the foundation of our rationality, and is its
> definite guarantee long before the dawn of any conscious
> generalization or syllogism. It is the function which no other
> animal shares. [1951, p. 70]

However important it may be for those involved in cartographic design and research to take into account the nature of the viewer as a constructive responder to visual sensation, the matter is not a simple one. Psychological theory still cannot account completely for man's behavior in this realm, and relevant experimental situations have accomplished even less to provide us with clear-cut analytical and prescriptive approaches. The material that follows, which examines physiological and psychological insights into visual cognition, varies somewhat in the degree of certainty that can be attached to it; but our general position will be clear and reasonably consistent, although at times it is based in belief and assumption, and at other times on behavioral, empirical laboratory evidence.

In looking, the eye is occupied with one of two kinds of movements. It may be momentarily fixating on a limited portion of the visual field, or it may be moving in jump fashion to a new portion of the field on which it will subsequently fixate. Information is taken in during the fixation, but little or none is obtained during the movement. The eye can shift to a new fixation point several times a second, and it is a source of wonder to those who study vision that the human being can integrate this shifting, continually moving flux of light patterns on the retina into the perception and conception of an object. There is virtually no solid information at present on exactly how this integration—or, as Neisser describes it, "translation"—from shifting light patterns to object conception takes place. As Lashley put it,

> Visual perceptions are rarely based upon a momentary stimu-
> lation of the fixed retina ... most of our perception of objects
> is derived from a succession of scanning movements, the
> succession of retinal images being translated into a single
> impression of form. [Neisser 1967, p. 139]

Neisser adds that "This act of 'translation' has hardly ever been studied, but it is evidently among the most fundamental cognitive processes." Much evidence has accumulated in the last century or so about persons who have been given eyesight by means of surgery. It is clear from the subjects' difficulties in "learning" to see that impressions of objects, or form, are *not* immediately, spontaneously given. The subjects generally report a blur of light and color; objects that they knew well by touch had to be re-learned as objects that could be seen.

Neisser's development of visual perception as a constructive act is worth examining in more detail. He believes the perceiver "makes" stable objects, using information from a number of visual "snapshots":

> Such a process requires a kind of memory, but not one which preserves pictorial copies of earlier patterns. Instead, there is a constantly developing schematic model, to which each new fixation adds new information. The individual "snapshots" are remembered only in the way that the words of a sentence are remembered when you recollect nothing but its meaning; they have contributed to something which endures. [1967, p. 140]

This "something which endures" is what Polanyi has referred to as tacit knowledge, that is, the nonverbal, non-imaged conception of meaning—that which is held to be true and known. Neisser feels that the process of visual integration or construction has been little studied because it is so efficient as to be undetectable in normal experience:

> Our eye movements generally have no counterpart in phenomenal experience. We are not aware of the succession of different inputs in our own perception, so the issue does not force itself upon us. It is the very unobtrusiveness of the movements that seems to demand explanation. The integrative process is so efficient that a radical realignment of the input several times each second can go completely unnoticed! [1967, p. 142]

It is not the eye itself that must be the primary focus of our attention in this analysis of visual cognition, because the function must largely be associated with the brain. As Neisser points out:

> It has been said that beauty is in the eye of the beholder. As a hypothesis about localization of function, the statement is not

quite right—the brain and not the eye is surely the most
important organ involved. Nevertheless it points clearly enough
toward the central problem of cognition. Whether beautiful
or ugly or just conveniently at hand, the world of experience is
produced by the man who experiences it. [1967, p. 3]

In line with this view of perception as a process of active construction, Neisser prefers the conception of "synthesizing a perceptual object" to that of "analyzing the input," and he is interested
in what he calls figural synthesis. Recent evidence indicates that this
position is correct, or at least compatible with other neurological
findings. Pribram (1969) describes research on animals and hypothe-
sizes that the hologram might constitute a useful model for the
storage of information in the brain. This hypothesis is particularly
interesting here because it suggests that what is stored is not the
initial perceptual object itself, but the *activity* of synthesizing the
object. In discussing the interference effects of standing wave fronts
in the brain, Pribram writes (p. 77):

How can interference effects be produced in the brain? . . .
The hypothesis presented here is that the totality of this process
has a more or less lasting effect on protein molecules and
perhaps other macromolecules at the synaptic junctions and
can serve as a neural hologram from which, given the appropriate input, an image can be *reconstructed.* [italics added]

This research was reported almost three years after Neisser wrote:

The notion of figural synthesis suggests one speculative possibility. What seems familiar is not the stimulus object after all,
but the perceived object. Perhaps we experience familiarity *to
the extent that the present act of visual synthesis is identical
to an earlier one.* [1967, p. 98]

One of the fundamental aspects of visual perception is the
perception, or as we argue here, the *construction* of shape. Shape is a
rather difficult concept to define, although in common experience
everyone knows what it is. A great deal of effort has been devoted to
attempts to develop useful numerical indices of shape, but so far
none seems to have been successful (Sanders and Porter 1974, p.
260). Even more difficult than its definition is the determination of
what it is about either a visual stimulus encounter or an experience
that provides the sensation of shape. Arnheim (1964) focuses sharply
on the latter when he describes the example of a man who follows

certain written directions as he walks, turns, continues in straight lines, then changes direction. When he has finished he will have traced out the contour of what might be a very familiar shape, say a cross. But he will have no idea of this shape from the experience of walking along its contour. Arnheim comments that "Although he has traced the entire contour, his experience is unlikely to have contained the essentials of what we see when we look at a cross-shaped design" (p. 62).

Arnheim's example is of particular relevance to the mapping process because it points up one of the unique attributes of mapping. Much of the "real world" milieu is difficult or impossible to observe visually, either for rather obvious reasons, such as man's diminutive size and the difficulty of access, or else because matters of interest such as bedrock character or land values are not necessarily visually observable. In mapping, one objective is to discover (by seeing) meaningful physical or intellectual shape organizations in the milieu, *structures that are likely to remain hidden until they have been mapped.* Such a shape organization might be defined as that figural quality attained by an array of points that could not have been predicted from simple point-to-point correspondence; "plotting out" or "mapping" is a method for searching for such meaningful designs. Phenomena in the milieu often achieve such a quality *only* in representation, rather than in direct experience. Thus, mapping provides an ordering or simplifying system that has great advantages over the direct experience of reality.

The construction of shape from visual stimulation is a remarkably efficient and elegant process.

> It was the merit of Gestalt psychology to make us aware of the remarkable performance involved in perceiving shapes. Take, for example, a ball or an egg: we can see their shapes at a glance. Yet suppose that instead of the impression made on our eye by an aggregate of white points forming the surface of an egg, we were presented with another, logically equivalent, presentation of these points as given by a list of their spatial co-ordinate values. It would take years of labour to discover the shape inherent in this aggregate of figures—provided it could be guessed at all. The perception of the egg from the list of co-ordinate values would, in fact, be a feat rather similar in nature and measure of intellectual achievement to the discovery of the Copernican system. [Polanyi 1946, p. 24]

The construction of shape from a series of point fixations is, of course, a visual–spatial process, with the two aspects hardly separable. Writing in a quite different context, Blanshard describes spatial synthesis as the "... power of turning the successive into coexistent parts of a pattern ... " (1948, 1:247), a process that is strikingly similar to Neisser's act of visual "translation" referred to earlier. This spatial synthesis is fundamental to the nature of map perception, and it is central to our discussion.

The Gestalt psychologists have been greatly interested in the spontaneous recognition of figures, or shapes, which took place as the viewer separated figure from ground in ordinary vision. On the basis of a great many experiments and more casual observations, they formulated principles that help to predict viewers' perceptions of graphic arrays. For example, they found that closed configurations will tend to be seen as figures more consistently than will open ones, that objects that are closer together will tend to form a new object or configuration, and so on. Further, the investigators discovered that the expectations of the subject viewing the display could have a marked effect on what was perceived. In reality, however, these principles turn out to be of limited utility, for most real objects tend to vary in all the figural characteristics the experimenters isolated. The question remains, therefore, as to which, if any, of the dimensions of the stimulus array will be most important in defining shape or figural qualities.

Up to this point the discussion has dealt with philosophical and psychological approaches to visual cognition that have general applicability—that is, the functioning of the system has been assumed to be independent of the nature of the phenomenon viewed. We shall now turn to a consideration of several visual processes that are particularly significant in understanding the nature of map perception/cognition. Even though such processes are germane to the observation of the general visual milieu, the more limited nature of the map display imposes particular constraints, and this enables us to be more precise in the description of the process.

Recently, a useful conception for cartography, the recognition of *different kinds of seeing* or different kinds of visual processing, has emerged simultaneously from two disparate sources. Research related to this notion has been conducted by psychologists and, quite independently, by a cartographer; both efforts attained nearly identical conclusions. The result has been to provide us with a tool for analyzing the hitherto only intuitively defined "visual hierarchy," which, in cartography, refers to the sequence of organization or figure perception that takes place when viewing a relatively complex display. We know that the viewer cannot simultaneously construct more than one figure out of such a display, and consequently, processing must take place in some kind of sequence.

Fundamentally, it is hypothesized on the basis of considerable empirical evidence that seeing, hearing, and remembering are all constructive acts which make more use or less of stimulus information (raw sensation) depending upon circumstances. It is further postulated that there are two stages in the processing of the stimuli: the first is fast, crude, holistic, and parallel (i.e., the same operation carried out simultaneously for a variety of stimuli or over a relatively extensive spatial field); the second is deliberate, attentive, detailed, and sequential. In vision, in the absence of a habitual pattern for fixation—for example, the reading of textual material—the first process seems to take in much of the display at a holistic or global level and seeks to construct major shapes; it functions in order to select the portions of the field that will be examined in more detail with the second process. During this first stage, the organism is deciding what to fixate next.

Evidence for this conception of staged processing has been accumulated primarily in terms of the different rates at which the processes take place. Neisser's research, as well as that of a number of his colleagues, has been conducted with search tasks which show, for example, that although a subject can examine the names in a telephone directory very rapidly and can determine that certain names are *not* the one he seeks, he has not actually *read* the names, in the usual sense of the word, because he cannot remember what names were rejected. In other words, there seems to be an initial, "pre-attentive" form of fast and efficient visual processing which allows one to reject non-target information, while the "focal-attentive" stage, the actual recognition of the target information, occurs as a consequence of a more thorough, deliberate, and slower process. There is more recent evidence in experimental psychology that the "pre-attentive" form of processing, as Neisser described it, is not quite as low-level a cognitive process as was originally thought. The phenomenon of target material "leaping out of the page" is common and well-documented, but as Posner (Chase 1973, p. 41) notes, "this phenomenological experience occurs rather late in the sequence of processing as a result of memory search and its occurence in Neisser's task cannot be used to infer that rejection of a letter is a low level process." Nevertheless, the basic observations on which this psychological processing model was based continue to be valid.

Neisser has shown that it takes no more time to search for five names than it does for one, an argument for parallel processing. When, however, the eye fixates on the target name and the subject wants to ascertain positively that a particular name is the one he is seeking, he processes portions of the name more sequentially and much more slowly. All of this is basic to developing a theory of pattern recognition that eliminates the many contradictions in visual perception research. Neisser comments:

> This means that the processes of pattern recognition are, after all, partly sequential. In giving up the hypothesis that all visual processing is *spatially* parallel, we necessarily introduce successive stages into our model of cognition, i.e., mechanisms which are not *operationally* parallel either. Attentive acts are carried out in the context of the more global properties already established at the preattentive level. In this way—and I think only in this way—can we understand the phenomena stressed by the Gestalt psychologists, many of which seem so out of place in modern theories based on parallel processing of features and parts. [1967, p. 90]

In some ways, this two-stage (pre-attentive/focal-attentive) theory is rather like the theory of molecular structure which finally reconciled the wave/solid-body-in-orbit points of view, when the two concepts originally seemed to exclude one another.

During the second, focal-attentive, stage the viewer can attend to only a single, limited portion of the field at any given moment. The figure that he constructs during this period of attention is partially dependent on the nature of the stimulus configuration (contrast levels, proximity, brightness, and all the factors that tend to produce "good figure," as they have been outlined by the Gestalt psychologists), but the construct is also partially determined by the viewer's own characteristics. Neisser (1967, p. 301) notes that "The course of synthesis is partly determined by stimulus information, but it also depends on such factors as past experience, expectation, and preference."

Among the common activities performed by a map percipient is looking for some particular representation on a map. One searches in the visual display for such things as familiar shapes, route numbers, or place names. Characteristically, some items are more easily found than others, but the percipient generally feels that the information *he* seeks should be found very rapidly. Thus task consideration is vitally important in the selection of marks in the design plan. This is exemplified, for example, in choosing the type for map use, because the names on the map are not "transparent"— they will not be read for meaning in the way that the sequential words in a sentence are read for a meaning that goes beyond the awareness of the words themselves. Rather, the percipient will seek and identify a target name in much the same manner that a child tries to find all the cats that are visually embedded in the drawing of a tree in a hidden-figure puzzle.

In order to obtain empirical information about the processes that are involved in name-finding on maps, a series of experiments was conducted by Bartz (1970). Maps were constructed in five colors, simulating a general reference map of a country of the type commonly found in popular atlases. All content and design factors were held constant, with the exception of the typeface used for about 140 names, which was varied in a number of ways. On some maps only one typeface was used; on others two or three faces were mixed. Subjects engaged in a timed search for six names in sequence. For the maps on which more than one typeface was used, there were two searching conditions: some of the subjects searched for the names after seeing them on a typewritten list; others searched from lists that showed the target names set in the same typeface in which they appeared on the map.

For the maps that contained only one typeface, it was found that the five typefaces were equivalent in their effect on average search time. The ease with which target names on a map can be searched for and found may be considered a form of cartographic legibility (Bartz 1969*b*). It took subjects approximately the same amount of time to search a map set in a serif face as it did to search a map set in a sans-serif or a bold face. Further, no difference in search speed was recorded between names set in upper and lower case, as compared to names set in all capitals. But when the maps contained names set in two or three distinctly different typefaces, the results of the search task experiment changed. For example, for maps with names set in different typefaces, search times were slowed *if* the subject did not know the face in which his particular target names would appear (that is, if he were searching for the names on a typewritten list). But if the subject was first shown the typeface in which the target name was set, his search time dropped markedly from the time taken to search from a typewritten list, in some cases by a factor of three.

When the data were analyzed more closely, it became apparent that search times from lists typeset to match the faces used on a map were roughly proportional to the number of names on the map that appeared in the same face as the target names. When the subjects were searching from typewritten lists, search time was proportional to the total number of names on the map, presumably because all map names had an equal probability of being a target name. It appeared, therefore, that a visual processing mechanism enabled the searcher to reject all names set in the "wrong" (non-target) face, with virtually no processing time, but that the "right" names had to be examined more slowly, in more detail. It is significant to note that the factor of three, by which the slower processing exceeded the faster processing, is similar to the figure arrived at independently, under different but related circumstances, by Beller (1968), a psychologist. It appears that this "constant" reflects a basic, widely operative phenomenon and is not just a special result of cartographic research.

The role of expectation thus becomes apparent as being significant in determining which portions of the map (or map names, in this case) will be attended to in great detail, and which can be more rapidly processed at a general level. It seems likely that at one time or another all map users have experienced the influence of expectation. One often looks for a name unsuccessfully, only to find it eventually in the area being searched, but somehow, because it looked different from what had been expected, the searcher's expectation caused him earlier to ignore it as not appropriate for more detailed inspection. The frustration of something "being there all the time, right under one's nose," is a common experience—too common with many maps, it appears.

The conception of different kinds of visual processing is clearly one element of seeing which is significant in any field of graphic presentation, and how research findings in this area could be utilized in cartography is readily apparent. We should know, for example, what kinds of visual differences (or coding dimensions) will permit rapid separation of the visual field into organized parts or categories, so that the map percipient can arrive at the portion that is the focus of his search with maximum efficiency. For example, would two categories of place names set in the same typeface be more quickly isolated from one another if they had a hue distinction, or a boldness distinction? How many categories of information can readily be sorted out at the preattentive level? Which graphic distinctions will speed the focal attentive processes? It is likely that search-time variations would provide the basis for establishing these distinctions.

A somewhat related matter is that of the concept of visual hierarchy and attendant aspects of visual cognition, topics that have gained the attention of some cartographers (Dent 1972). Although visual hierarchy is relatively difficult to define verbally, it is an easy notion to grasp if one looks at almost any map. The viewer cannot simultaneously apprehend everything about the graphic display. Some shape, mark, color, or contrast is perceived first, another second, and so on. There will occur, therefore, a sequence of visual processing that appears to be at least partially determined by the graphic characteristics of the display, such as the degree of contrast, color saturation, complexity, or whatever the dominant features may be (Jenks 1973). The preattentive process fixes the eye on an element that is then further processed to the point where some aspect of it is recognizable. It is likely that the viewer will unconsciously associate the sequence of processing with a sequence of "importance"; that is, the aspects of the map that are apprehended first will be construed as most striking or most important, and are therefore likely to be most distinctly remembered. These notions of *separability* and *memorability* of the display are fundamental considerations for the mapmaker in determining the graphic character of the map elements.

In a limited study bearing upon the notion of visual hierarchy, the differential attention-getting characteristics of map elements and their consequent memorability were analyzed (Bartz 1967). Although the methodology of the study was highly experimental, it seemed reasonably efficient; despite the need for considerably more work in this area, the outcome appears to be valuable. Children were asked to look at several four-color political reference maps of one of the states of the United States, and to describe the maps in various ways. They were asked what elements were most attention-getting, how one map differed in appearance from another map, and so on. It was thought that the subjects' spontaneous responses and their vocabulary would provide useful information about what was noticed (or, from another point of view, what vocabulary they had available for description, a factor that strongly affects what will be remembered). The hypothesis proved to be true; a reasonable amount of consistency among the subjects was recorded, and the consensus about design choices was similar to that obtained from a group of graphically sophisticated artists and designers; the latter group's predictions about the impact and effect of specific design choices were largely fulfilled.

After the general questioning was completed, one of the maps was removed, and the subject (who had not been told previously that this would be part of the experiment) was asked to describe what he remembered of the map. The items that were remembered, or considered important enough to describe, were surprisingly consistent. Moreover, the sequences in which map features were described did not differ greatly from one subject to another. Thus it was concluded that this tentative work provided considerable evidence of a fairly stable visual hierarchy of map perception.

Certain graphic characteristics of the maps tested in this study were observed to have strong effects on the seeing process in its formation of a visual hierarchy. The reciprocal relation of figure and ground is clearly of fundamental concern. We appear to make sense of displays—or of the real world, for that matter—primarily as we are able to establish meaningful shapes, and apparently this striving for meaning in shapes can be helped or hindered by the character of their graphic representation (color, texture, etc.), as well as by their arrangement. Presumably, certain shapes can be made to dominate or to recede, or all shapes can be made equal in dominance, or of equal non-dominance (a condition aptly described by one of the children in the study as making the map "blur-ish"). A road network, for example, might be subdued visually so that it could be seen only when actively looked for. On the other hand, it might be desirable to have it emerge whole, *as* a network, much as the blood vessels on a diagram of body circulation might be made to emerge as a coherent system. As another example, all the countries on a political map could be shown in colors of "equal" dominance, or some could be seen as darker or brighter—dominant in some respect. All of these conceptions related to the notion of visual hierarchy seem, typically, not to have received much attention in map design or map research. When Williams says (1956, p. 4): "The word symbol becomes a value symbol when its size or style is meant to show the relative importance of the city or the coalfield," he overlooks the fact of "seeing" that every mark on the map, whether it is *meant* to or not, takes on a value in the percipient's conception (Robinson 1970). It is erroneous to assume that graphic elements are "valueless," unless we make them otherwise.

There now exists a sizable body of published psychological research into the effect of coding dimensions (the graphic form given to a symbol—color, shape, size, etc.) on various tasks involving the use of graphic displays. Very little of this research, however, has been conducted in the context of cartography, probably because of the enormous complexity of even a simple map. Much of this research has focused on the coding dimensions of the hue and value (brightness) of color areas, and on the shape and size of symbols. The findings indicate that the effect of these dimensions seems to depend to an appreciable extent on the nature of the task in which they become a consideration. For example, at some times color is the most effective coding dimension, at other times shape, and at still others size. The differences between color and shape perception, and the different ways that color and shape affect the viewer, have long been subjects of philosophical and psychological interest, and definitive answers to questions about them are not yet available. In view of the two basic kinds of visual processing discussed previously, we suggest some hypotheses as examples to illustrate the relevance to cartography of the fundamental characteristics of seeing. The experience of color often seems the most spontaneous aspect of any visual encounter. It can be conjectured that this might be so because a color area is unitary and totally redundant within itself; and therefore it requires less constructive activity on the part of the viewer. It is likely, therefore, that a color area normally can be rapidly processed in its entirety at the preattentive level. Shape, on the other hand, seems usually more complex within itself; and the more complex an image is, the longer it takes to synthesize, according to Neisser's conception of figural synthesis. More activity would be required, therefore, to construct a recognizable shape than to process an area of homogeneous color, which would account for the apparent spontaneity of the response to color.

Although this discussion of the seeing process has focused on the importance of the characteristics of a graphic array as determinants of the order in which aspects of the map are seen and remembered, we cannot ignore the influence on perception wielded by attitudes and knowledge brought to the viewing task by the map percipient. Neisser's description of the two ways of processing visual sensation should be set alongside another conception of seeing, somewhat related but nevertheless distinct, developed by Polanyi, who is concerned with the perception or construction of part/whole or figure/ground relationships in a way that relates to and elaborates the position the Gestaltists developed.

The process of comprehending, of understanding, of acquiring tacit knowledge is seen by Polanyi to be a "grasping of disjointed parts into a comprehensive whole" (1959, p. 28). He points out that the Gestalt psychologists have been studying this phenomenon for decades, but have, he feels, missed the point in viewing the perception of wholes, of *Gestalten,* as passive experiences, without realizing that such perception represents a method for acquiring knowledge:

> We cannot comprehend a whole without seeing its parts, but we
> can see the parts without comprehending a whole. Thus we
> may advance from a knowledge of the parts to the under-
> standing of the whole. This comprehension may be effortless or
> difficult, indeed, so difficult that its achievement will represent
> a discovery. Yet we shall acknowledge the same comprehending
> faculty at work in all cases. Once comprehension is achieved, we
> are not likely to lose sight again of the whole; yet comprehen-
> sion is not completely irreversible. By looking very closely at the
> several parts of the whole, we may succeed in diverting our
> attention from the whole and even lose sight of it altogether.
> [p. 29]

In comprehending the whole, the attention shifts from a concern with the particulars to an understanding of their joint meaning. To see the whole we must see the parts, but the manner in which we see the parts has changed. Polanyi refers to the two ways we see things as *subsidiary awareness* and *focal awareness.* When the whole is apprehended, there is focal awareness of the whole and only subsidiary awareness of the particulars. The reverse is generally true when the particulars are the subject of attention, although there may be focal awareness of the parts with no awareness whatsoever of the whole.

There is a striking description of this shift from focal to subsidiary awareness in John Updike's novel *Rabbit, Run* (1960). Appro-priately, it concerns map use. At one point as the man, Rabbit, is driving aimlessly, he looks at a map in confusion and fatigue in order to find out where he is:

> Rabbit puts the shift in neutral and pulls out the emergency
> brake and turns on the roof light and studies the map. . . . He

has forgotten the numbers of the routes he has taken and the names of the towns he has passed through. He remembers Frederick but can't find it and in time realizes he is searching in a section due west of Washington where he has never been. There are so many red lines and blue lines, long names, little towns, squares and circles and stars. He moves his eyes north but the only line he recognizes is the straight dotted line of the Pennsylvania–Maryland border. . . . He burns his attention through the film fogging his eyes down into the map again. At once "Frederick" pops into sight, but in trying to steady its position he loses it. . . . The names melt away and he sees the map whole, a net, all those red lines and blue lines and stars, a net he is somewhere caught in. [pp. 33–34]

This passage illustrates the fact that a viewer can have an awareness *either* of discrete parts—of stars, of lines, *or* of the whole—of the network; there cannot be awareness of both at the same time. Clearly we are describing the figure-ground phenomenon the Gestalt psychologists have presented so convincingly, although not accounted for. Any map has the potential for being seen as many layers or units of figure on a variety of grounds. A map percipient must cope with visually embedded and intertwined figures of rather great complexity, and often he succeeds only because a number of major shapes, such as country areas, land masses, or water bodies are highly familiar to educated adults.

When figures emerge almost spontaneously on maps, as familiar shapes do, it is because percipients have had many years of experience in constructing them, not because they must invariably be perceived as such. Before a figure can emerge whole, as a unit, one must, presumably, at first encounter, actively trace its contour, holding the pieces or fixations until the whole somehow "clicks" into view as a unit with shape. As we have indicated, the speed with which this happens varies with both the graphic character of the display and the experiences and psychological makeup of the viewer.

With this understanding of the seeing process, it becomes clear that virtually no graphic element of a map can be considered in isolation. All figure-ground and part-whole relations appear to be reciprocal and reversible, because they are based on alterations in attention. There may, of course, be high probabilities associated with certain situations—X may more often be seen as figure than Y, but a shift in awareness or a shift in the purpose for which a map is approached may cause X to become part of a larger figure, or even to become ground. Most map users are familiar with the disorientation experienced when the water areas of a map (instead of the land shapes) are seen as figure. The shape of the Mediterranean Sea around the peninsula of Italy is not generally a familiar figure. When it is seen as such, because design characteristics lead to its being seen as figure rather than as more familiar ground, the very familiar peninsular shape can itself become a meaningless, unrecognizable shape. This can also happen to the shapes of thematic distributions and to country shapes in relation to one another.

To conclude this summary of the basic aspects of seeing involved in map perception, it is appropriate to emphasize the complexity of the map-viewer transaction. This involves such fundamentals as that the particular graphic elements of the map will have specific effects, that the arrangement of these elements, with respect to all others, will have others, and finally that the visual-cognitive acts of construction through which the viewer engages the map will induce still others. The phrase "seeing a map" gives simplistic verbal unity to what is in reality a complex, multidimensional process, which needs considerably greater explication and clarification than investigators have yet been able to give it.

5 The Conception of Space

... what is first in order of nature may be last in the order of explicit knowledge.
Brand Blanshard

Earlier we emphasized that a fundamental characteristic of mapping is that the map is actually a diminutive reproduction of the real space to which it refers. To be sure, the map space is always a transformation of the referent space; the alteration may range from being either negligible or purposefully extreme, but in any case the map *is* space. Although this may seem obvious, it is important: it is unlikely that even disinterested map viewers will not react in some fashion to the map space, and by definition map percipients will interact with it. How they do so, of course, is a function of fundamental human concepts of space.

All functioning human beings show evidence of possessing spatial concepts and abilities. In the first chapter we saw that students attempting to understand other kinds of knowledge or symbolic activity often concluded that spatial experience is *the* basic experience. It is obviously necessary to consider the nature of spatial knowledge—cognitive spatial operations as well as thought about space as a construct—in order to understand the transformation from experience to symbol that mapping represents. This is an exceedingly difficult topic to analyze and discuss, because everything that is "known" about spatial knowledge must be derived from observations of external behavior. Consequently, statements about the nature of spatial constructs and spatial understanding, at best, must be made in an "as if" form; behavior can be explained *as if* the individual behaving in a particular way has a particular internal spatial schema, *as if* he has a particular spatial image, or *as if* he has a particular body of beliefs about relations in space. As the comparison of mapping and verbal language has shown, there can be no direct or simple translation from images to words; consequently, since our concern with spatial concepts relates largely to presentational forms, even the development of a vocabulary to conduct discourse about it is a formidable task. But unless we try to understand the nature of the knowledge that we *develop* through the operation of mapping and that we *reflect* by what we choose to put on maps and how we choose to do it, our attempt to analyze the fundamental nature of cartography would be incomplete.

Blanshard's observation (1948, 1:525) that "what is first in order of nature may be last in the order of explicit knowledge" refers to our knowledge of space and time, although what he says applies equally well to other aspects of reality. He continues: "Time and space are only examples taken arbitrarily. What has been said about them could be said of all manner of qualities and relations present in perception, but grasped only implicitly." The conversion of our implicit, common experience in space to the constructs we group under the general heading of "spatial knowledge," and the fundamental way in which these constructs relate to the activity of mapping, form the topic of this chapter.

Our ideas about space do not develop at the same time or in the same way as do our abilities to perceive and operate in space:

> But space as it first appears to us is so inextricably one with
> what fills it that the clear distinction of the two comes only with
> development and effort . . . Indeed it was probably long after
> geometrical devices had been used for laying out and dividing
> land that the notion ever suggested itself of abstracting and
> studying these for their own sake. And here the history of
> the race. . . . We think space before we think *of* it, and we
> think of it in a matrix of irrelevancy long before we think of it
> pure. [Blanshard, pp. 524–25]

Our approach in analyzing the character of spatial knowledge in this chapter is that of "the history of the individual," and to do this we will lean heavily upon the ontogenetic origins of representational space as developed by Piaget and his associates at the Jean Jacques Rousseau Institute in Geneva, Switzerland. It must be stressed that our emphasis, like theirs, is not with perceptual space but with representational space; we are not concerned with the physiological and psychological factors associated with the development of perceptions of objects and phenomena in space, or with the ways that actual operations and activities are carried out in space. Rather, we shall concentrate on the representational aspects, that is, on the development of the ability to visualize, to form images, to deal with systems of relations in space in the absence of the perceptual stimuli themselves. This is the contrast between actually perceiving and doing in space, as opposed to being able to perform spatial operations conceptually. Clearly, a comprehension of mapping involves all these notions. The cartographer who understands the possible internal schemas of space that map percipients bring to his map will have diagnostic, if not prescriptive, tools, available to him.

The most comprehensive experimentation and theory development in the realm of conceptual space is that carried out over a considerable period under the general direction of Piaget. Whenever the name "Piaget" is used throughout the following material, it really refers to Piaget, Inhelder, and a number of associates at the Institute. In their work with children, they are concerned with more fundamental issues than the simple description of the child's abilities to conceive of and deal with space. Their investigations were focused upon the nature of space itself: whether it truly is an innate idea, an outcome of experience in the physical world, or whether it is a construction resulting from the operations carried out by the individual. Piaget and his associates went about this investigation primarily through the method of clinical work with children who were interviewed and observed individually from birth through late adolescence. Although spontaneous behavior was recorded, emphasis was placed on semistructured experiments in which the children were given materials in spatial situations and asked to perform particular tasks involving manipulation of objects, to verbalize about them, or to produce drawings or other representational systems. The same tasks were given to the same children over a number of years; the same tasks were also given to children of different ages, at one time. From inferences based on such experimental data, they constructed an intricate, comprehensive theory that could account for children's conceptions of space as they developed toward maturation. Following is a condensed summary of the hypothesized stages of this development. A few major ideas can be summarized first, then elaborated upon.

Conceptions of representational space trail behind the development of perceptual space, that is, there may be a lag of many years between the time a child can successfully act upon a particular perceived aspect of space and the time he can represent or use a representation of such aspects. In this connection, it is important to note that there probably are a great many individuals who never do develop a facility for dealing with representational space in a systematic way, though they may function well enough perceptually in the presence of real situations or objects. Furthermore, it appears that the conception of space by the average child develops sequentially, from the simple, basic topological relationships to the more difficult conceptions of projective and Euclidean space. Again, it is noteworthy that, as in the conceptualization of other matters, it is in the nature of things that not every individual attains the same level of sophistication. It is this developmental conception of space that we will consider in detail, for only by understanding the human being's ability to use and understand representations of space will we understand the percipient's ability to interact with maps. Mapping represents a way or ways of thinking about space, not just dealing with it directly in perceptual terms.

One's understanding of spatial representation has its foundation in the early development of spatial perception. Piaget outlines the development of spatial relationships as perceived during the first eighteen months of life, and finds that a number of relations are involved during the earliest constructions of perceptual space.

First is the idea of propinquity, or *proximity*. Piaget, in the area of visual perception, says (Piaget and Inhelder 1967, p. 6):

> The most elementary spatial relationship which can be grasped by perception would seem to be that of "proximity," corresponding to the simplest type of perceptual structurization, [*sic*] namely, the "nearby-ness" of elements belonging to the same perceptual field.

A second idea that develops is that of *separation*. In early perception two nearby elements may be partly blended and confused. An act of separation is required to dissociate them. A third spatial relationship present in elementary perception is that of surrounding or *enclosure*. Another fundamental relationship (p. 7) "... is established when two neighboring though separate elements are ranged one before another. This is the relation of *order* (or spatial succession)." Moreover, there appears to be one particularly important variant in the relation of order: the idea of symmetry, or double order. Finally, there is the relationship of continuity, though it appears to be some time before the perceptual field may be considered a continuous whole. For a long time in infancy, the spaces that are qualitatively experienced (whether by tactile, visual, or other means) are not coordinated among themselves, and it may be that continuity has a different character at different levels of development. In any event, Piaget is firmly convinced that continuity is constructed, not given. All these relationships may be considered as topological: they deal with relations and equivalences of being bounded or connected rather than with those of size, shape, distance, angularity, or straightness.

During subsequent stages in an infant's development (up to about the age of one year), the handling of objects and other activities lead to the ability to construct figures mentally, and to the development of the idea of perceptual constancy in shape and size. Eventually, objects are recognized as being the same even when seen from different points of view and handled in different ways. This gives to objects a solidity and permanence they did not have during the earliest perceptions of simple topological relationships. Piaget believes that the development of the ability to perceive figures is rooted in sensorimotor activity, including eye movements, tactile exploration, imitating, active transpositions, and so on. Thus, according to Piaget, during this early period the principal perceptual forms (lines, circles, angles, etc.) are constructed or assembled from a wide variety of experiences.

From the beginning of the child's second year, Piaget reports that sensorimotor activity is

> enriched by systematic observation and enquiry, by tentative efforts at experimentation, and finally by fully intelligent practical activity through the internal co-ordination of relationships. . . . Whereas the achievements of the second period are essentially relative to the shape and dimensions of objects, those of the third period consist in bringing out the relationships of objects to each other. [Piaget and Inhelder 1967, p. 12]

Finally, during the latter stages of this period (between one and two years) there comes into being for the first time the *mental image,* which makes delayed imitation possible; as a result of this, there are the first attempts at drawing, or the beginning of the acquisition of the symbolic function. For the child, then, space has become somewhat representational.

From a rather early age the child is able to perceive things projectively (i.e., ordered from a single point of view) and to grasp certain metric relationships by perception alone, but it is some time before he can deal with perspective in thought, or perform the measuring operation on objects. In fact, it is not "until after seven to eight years of age that the measurement, conceptual co-ordination of perspective, understanding of proportions, etc., result in the construction of a conceptual space marking a real advance on perceptual space" (Piaget and Inhelder 1967, p. 13). Piaget stresses repeatedly that in the development of the notions of space, both static images, such as conjuring up a triangle or line, and the system of operations or motor transformations that may be applied to them are inextricably linked:

> And from this standpoint there can be no movement occurring in any conceivable type of behaviour which does not rest on perception. Neither can there be a perception taking place without activity which involves motor elements. It is the total "sensorimotor schema" which must constitute the starting point for the analysis of behaviour, and not perception or movement considered in isolation. [p. 14]

He further stresses the differences between perception and representation:

> Perception is the knowledge of objects resulting from direct contact with them. As against this, representation or imagination involves the evocation of objects in their absence or, when it runs parallel to perception, in their presence. [p. 17]

He sees shape, for example, as being abstracted from the object by virtue of actions the subject performs on the object, not as a direct, given result of simple perception. Drawing, too, is not only the expression of the visually or tactilely perceived referent, it is also the expression of the perceptual activity itself—a combination of the movements, anticipations, reconstructions, comparisons, etc., that accompany perception:

> Like a mental image, a drawing is an internal or external imitation of the object and not just a perceptual "photograph," whilst by its very nature imitation has the effect of prolonging the muscular accommodation or adaptation involved in perceptual activity. [p. 33]

Thus the construction of space begins on the perceptual level and continues on the representational one. During this early period of drawing, the child recognizes and draws only shapes that are closed and rounded, based on his acquisition of the basic topological notions, such as openness, closure, proximity, surrounding, etc. These relations express the simplest possible coordination of actions, and therefore are the first to appear in the child's development. By the age of six or seven, however, the child has developed the ability to recognize shapes and figures in situations where conceptions of metric and projective space are involved.

Piaget extends the exploration of the path of spatial development by investigating "pictorial space," the relationships children use in their drawings. He warns:

> A drawing is a representation, which means that it implies the construction of an image, which is something altogether different from perception itself, and there is no evidence that the spatial relationships of which this image is composed are on the same plane as those revealed by the corresponding perception. A child may see the nose above the mouth, but when he tries to conjure up these elements and is no longer really perceiving them, he is liable to reverse their order, not simply from want of skill in drawing or lack of attention, but also and more precisely, from the inadequacy of the instruments of spatial representation which are required to reconstruct the order along the vertical axis. [Piaget and Inhelder 1967, p. 47]

In studying children's spontaneous drawings, Piaget examines three stages of development from the point of view of spatial representation: (1) synthetic incapacity, (2) intellectual realism, and (3) visual realism. During the first stage, the child's drawing may exhibit the weakness noted above, where his perceptions and representational abilities are not matched. Only the simplest topological relationships are retained here; projective relationships (perspectives with projections and sections) and Euclidean relationships (proportions and distances) are neglected.

During the second stage of intellectual realism, the child draws not what he actually sees of the object, but everything that he knows is there. Piaget finds that this stage provides evidence of a type of spatial awareness in which Euclidean and projective relationships are just beginning to emerge. Coordinated points of view are lacking, although different parts of the picture may share a particular point of view. Different sides of objects are shown, for they are known to appear with different points of view. These "pseudo-rotations" disappear at about age seven or eight, at the same time that the child begins to grasp real projective relations. Piaget notes:

> Thus with this kind of drawing [that is, done during this stage], resemblance to the model amounts to no more than a crude sort of "homeomorphism"; that is to say, a point-point, term for term correspondence, remaining purely intuitive and qualita-

tive without any co-ordination of projective or metrical relationships, although these begin to be separated out within the topological complex. [Piaget and Inhelder 1967, p. 51]

Finally Piaget finds that at about age eight or nine the child produces a type of drawing that tries to take into account perspective, proportions, and distance all at the same time. This is the period of "visual realism."

In concluding this portion of the analysis, Piaget stresses that geometrical space is not just a "tracing" made over a physical space, which temporarily corresponds to it on a point-by-point basis. Rather,

> The abstraction of shape actually involves a complete reconstruction of physical space, made on the basis of the subject's own actions and to that extent, based originally upon a sensorimotor, and ultimately on a mental, representational space determined by the co-ordination of these actions. . . . From beginning to end of the process just recapitulated, all these structures are invariably derived from the general co-ordination of physical actions. [Piaget and Inhelder 1967, p. 77]

The reconstruction of shapes requires an active process of "putting in relation to," thus implying that the abstraction of shape is based on the child's own actions and comes about through their gradual coordination.

By studying forms of children's behavior other than drawings, such as arranging objects in various kinds of order or analyzing knots, Piaget reaches a number of important conclusions. He finds, for example, that the most fundamental characteristic of the actions by which a child *generates* (not just perceives) the notion of space is expressed through the relationship of proximity. By observing his subjects as they arrange objects as directed, Piaget finds that by about age six or seven they arrive at what he considers a stable and rational conception of direct and reverse order. He also finds this conception to be no more a product of abstraction from direct perception of the object than were the earlier relations of proximity, separation, etc. Instead,

> Order is abstracted through increasing co-ordination of actions such as transferring (transporting elements mentally) and replacing, step by step and piece by piece. It is a result of reconstructing the object through ordered actions, and not a

directly abstracted quality. The physical order found in the object is reproduced through the adaptation of these actions, which in consequence lie at the root of the geometrical concept of order. [Piaget and Inhelder 1967, p. 103]

Another important consideration is the development of different notions of continuity. How does the child pass from simple perceptual or intuitive continuity to conceptual or operational continuity so that he can integrate the notions of proximity, separation, order, and surrounding into an organized whole? Piaget finds the most critical period of this development to be from about seven to twelve years of age, and studies it in various ways during that time.

since it is part of our aim to show that . . . in its mathematical connotation the idea of continuity is far from being a simple fact of experience, but actually develops from perception to concrete operations of thought, it seems relevant to test our theories by applying them to this particular concept. Now the mind does not pass directly from perceptual notions of continuity to abstract schemata evolved for the purpose of formulating such a notion. On the contrary, to arrive at reciprocal schemata of the sort required in order to reduce a line or surface to points and then reassemble the points to form a line or surface once more, necessitates the development of a complete mental structure. [Piaget and Inhelder 1967, p. 125]

Piaget concludes that in watching the child evolve the idea of continuity, one is watching the synthesis of all the topological relationships worked out by the child prior to this time:

In so far as operational subdivision involves a conceptual separation of neighboring points in place of a perceptual or intuitive process, it reconciles the opposing notions of proximity and separation within a global, unified concept of continuity. And in so far as it fills in the immediate surroundings of every point, continuity enables the operations of order and enclosure to find a general form equally applicable to lines, surfaces, and three-dimensional spaces. [p. 149]

Piaget then considers the development of projective and Euclidean notions of space, with the major difference between these and the psychologically more primitive topological notions occurring in the way in which different figures or objects are related to one another. Topological relations furnish the basis for a perceptual analysis that can consider each figure only in comparative isolation, rather than as part of a comprehensive system in which one can coordinate all possible figures into a comprehensive whole.

Projective and Euclidean space provide general systems of organization; objects and configurations may be located with respect to one another in accordance with general projective or perspective systems, or according to coordinate axes. The presence of such an organizing system makes possible the preservation of straight lines, angles, curves, and distances throughout various transformations, and as Piaget notes (Piaget and Inhelder 1967, p. 153) "Projective or euclidean structures are therefore much more complex in organization and are only evolved at a later stage in the child's development." He goes on to observe (pp. 153–54):

> Projective space ... begins psychologically at the point when the object or pattern is no longer viewed in isolation, but begins to be considered in relation to a "point of view." This is either the viewpoint of the subject, in which case a perspective relationship is involved, or else that of other objects on which the first is projected. Thus from the outset, projective relationships presume the inter-co-ordination of objects separated in space, as opposed to the internal analysis of isolated objects by means of topological relationships.

The selection of a particular point of view is critical in this process. The child's discovery that he has a particular viewpoint is far more difficult to achieve than might be supposed. To isolate his own point of view, he must be able to coordinate all possible points of view, then recognize one particular one as his own. The concept of the straight line develops in the child through the act of taking aim, or sighting, giving the simple idea of perspective.

For Piaget, this discovery that the straight line is actually constructed, not perceived, argues against a point of view that ascribes the origin of projective geometry to the influence of visual perception. This is

> to overlook the fact that the purely perceptual point of view is always completely egocentric. This means that it is both unaware of itself and incomplete, distorting reality to the extent that it remains so. As against this, to discover one's own viewpoint is to relate it to other viewpoints, to distinguish it from and co-ordinate it with them. Now perception is quite unsuited to this task, for to become conscious of one's own viewpoint is really to liberate oneself from it. To do this requires a system

of true mental operations, that is, operations which are reversible and capable of being linked together. [Piaget and Inhelder 1967, p. 193]

One of the ways in which children's ability to coordinate perspectives was studied employed a model landscape that included three mountains and a number of other objects. The subjects were shown photographs taken from different positions and asked to move a doll to the point from which they thought the picture had been taken. By about the age of eight or nine, most of the children could give nearly correct answers. From this study Piaget draws a number of conclusions, the major one (Piaget and Inhelder 1967, p. 244) being that "comprehensive co-ordination of viewpoints is the basic prerequisite in constructing simple projective relations." In addition, a major distinction between topological space and projective space is evident in the quite different ways in which mental operations superimpose themselves on perceptions, that is, the way children integrate perceptual data. Piaget observes:

> Topological space is wholly inherent to the object and consists of operations worked out step by step. It therefore corresponds to no more than a series of possible perceptions capable of being juxtaposed, and the main task of such operations is to assemble the data of this space into one coherent whole. . . . In contrast to this, a system of projective relations or perspective viewpoints consists essentially of operations which do not merely assemble perceptual data, but co-ordinate it in terms of reciprocal relationships. Hence the function of projective space is not to link up the various parts of the object, but to link together all the innumerable projections of it. [p. 244]

At one point, Piaget distinguishes between two kinds of geometry in a way that has particular relevance to cartography. The concept of "object geometry" implies objects being oriented relative to one another and to a system of reference points arranged along different dimensions. The object is measured as if the observer adhered directly to the surface or the interior of the object itself. In contrast to this, a "geometry of viewpoints" assumes that the object is envisaged not from its surface or interior, but from a more remote vantage point. In other words, the object is perceived from a particular point of view, or is located somewhere on the visual plane (perspective). The similarity of this distinction to a comparison of the earth as object, versus objects-on-the-earth, is obvious.

In studying children's ability to deal with the development and rotation of surfaces, Piaget observed for the first time the development of images that are beyond any one immediate perception:

> the notion of a developed solid is not a direct outcome of ordinary perception. Even the perception of all six sides of a solid such as a cube is not in itself sufficient to produce a mental image of the six sides rotated into one plane. What lies between the perception of a solid and the image of its plane rotation is an action, a motor response to perception. Thus, the image is a pictorial anticipation of an action not yet performed, a reaching forward from what is presently perceived to what may be, but is not yet perceived. [Piaget and Inhelder 1967, p. 294]

Very young children cannot form a mental image of how to unfold a piece of paper and must actually perform the action before they can predict how the object will appear when unfolded or rotated. Piaget finds that the child's image is more than a simple pictorial static copy of the object. Rather (p. 294) it is "an internalized act of imitation, a copy or transfer, not of the object as such, but of the motor response required to bring action to bear upon the object." This theme recurs throughout Piaget's work: intelligent thought is the product of a combination of the images of objects and the actions, real and potential, that may be brought to bear upon them. Actions give images flexibility and take them beyond direct perception.

Among the cartographer's most basic assumptions is the notion of the universal utility of coordinate systems of reference. It is sobering to note, however, that the ability to think in terms of coordinates appears to be the ultimate in the development of the conception of space. Piaget presents the rationale for the late development of this capacity as follows:

> As distinct from elementary topological relations which are concerned simply with the object as a thing in itself and with its various features taken in turn, we have shown that projective concepts imply a comprehensive linking together of figures in a single system, based on the co-ordination of a number of different viewpoints. But side by side with the development of this organized complex of viewpoints there also takes place a co-ordination of objects as such. This leads ultimately to the idea of euclidean space, the concepts of parallels, angles and proportion providing the transition between the two systems. Such a co-ordination of objects naturally assumes the conservation of

distance, together with the evolution of the notion of "displacement" or congruent transformation of spatial figures, culminating in the construction of systems of reference, or coordinates. [Piaget and Inhelder 1967, p. 357]

Piaget recognizes that many adults are so accustomed to using reference systems and organizing activities in empirical space by means of coordinate axes that they have difficulty recognizing that considerable learning must take place (usually between the ages of four and ten) before such habits are developed. Such learning cannot be taken for granted, or dismissed as self-evident:

> Here we touch on one of the worst misconceptions which has plagued the theory of geometrical concepts. From the fact that the child breathes, digests and possesses a heart that beats we do not conclude that he has any idea of alimentary metabolism or the circulatory system. At the very most he may have noticed his movements in breathing, or felt his pulse. But such perceptual-motor awareness does not lead to any understanding of the internal phenomena of which these movements are only the outward and visible sign. Similarly, from the fact that he can stand up or lie flat, the child at first derives only a strictly empirical awareness of the two postures and nothing more. To superimpose upon this a more general schema he must at some point go outside the purely postural field and compare his own position with those of surrounding objects, and this is something beyond purely empirical knowledge. [p. 378]

Although Piaget and his colleagues did not experiment with maps as such, they did conduct extensive investigations using diagrammatic layouts, including that of a model village. In the discussion of these observations, we find analytical concepts that seem to be of fundamental importance in understanding some of the logical assumptions that go into both making and interacting with maps. Consequently, we will examine these in some detail.

Young children, up to about age four, when shown a model display and then asked to arrange objects to replicate it, generally cannot do so. The explanation for their inability seems to have its origin in the two different ways the relationships among a group of objects may be treated. These relationships have been named by Piaget and his co-workers as (1) logico-mathematical and (2) spatio-temporal. In trying to account for the children's confusion, Piaget stresses the difference between the two:

> The former deal with groups of objects solely in terms of resemblances and differences between their members (i.e. in terms of logical classes, relations or numbers), whereas the latter deal with objects as such, whether simple or complex (groups of objects being treated as complex objects within a single configuration). [Piaget and Inhelder 1967, p. 430]

The assemblage of objects in the display whose arrangement the child was asked to copy may be considered to consist of either a logico-mathematical set (classes or numerical collections of objects) or of a spatial set (objects within a single configuration); to be successful at replicating the model, a child would have to envisage both of these aspects at the same time. As Piaget puts it, "the objects must be identical (logical correspondence) and arranged in an identical pattern (spatial correspondence)" (p. 430). A number of children grouped all of the objects in their replica in one corner, an action that Piaget feels indicates an inability to distinguish between spatial and logical relatedness.

The origin of logico-mathematical relations lies in the concepts of resemblance or difference, and the origin of spatio-temporal relations lies in the notions of proximity or separation. Before about age four, children seem unable to distinguish between these two classes—between spatial proximity as one form of relationship and logical resemblance as another. Gradually children learn to consider objects and relations from both of these points of view, and during the period from four to seven they show some progress in grouping small collections of objects, although general relationships of all objects are not yet clear. By age seven or eight, they have acquired most projective and Euclidean relationships and can make fairly successful replicas and drawings of the model. Measurements and reductions to scale, however, have not yet been mastered. These develop next, along with the notion of coordinate systems (rather than mere item-for-item matching) and by the age of eleven or twelve, children can successfully diagram the model layout. Piaget points out that this accomplishment is the result of a long sequence of encounters with ideas and the application of them in practical situations:

> It is clear that the knowledge acquired at school and exhibited in these replies is integrated with the whole body of concepts whose

development has been revealed in the course of the preceding experiments. For in truth, no learning can take place except by assimilation to existing schemata. Just as the child can draw long before he receives drawing lessons, so in the course of his daily life, he develops a body of concepts dealing with co-ordinates, perspectives, and similarities or proportions. It is this which enables him, at a particular age, to crystallize this system of practical operations around various new ideas which he encounters at school. [Piaget and Inhelder 1967, pp. 445–46]

In concluding his analysis, Piaget examines the distinction between the nature of (1) logico-mathematical (or logico-arithmetical) operations which lead to what Piaget calls "logical classification," on the one hand, and (2) spatio-temporal operations which lead to "infra-logical" or "sub-logical" classification, on the other. It is worth noting here that the implications of these terms in English translation are misleading, and it should be clearly understood that the prefixes "infra" and "sub" do not in any respect connote any lesser degree of significance or complexity, any more than they do in "infrared" or "subglacial." It is also worth noting that in all of Piaget's thinking the operations precede the idea; the act of seriation precedes the notion of a series, order is achieved only by ordering, separations by separating, and so on. By extension, then, we can see that mapping precedes the map and is logically prior to it. This provides the rationale for a detailed examination of the processes of mapping prior to any consideration of the map itself—except as one might infer the mapping processes from an examination of the product.

Piaget points out that concrete operations of a logico-arithmetical (logical) character deal solely with similarities and differences between discrete objects in a system that is a discontinuous whole, and are independent of the spatio-temporal location of the objects. Logical operations tend to produce collections of objects, and all classification systems, including number systems, are of this nature. Exactly parallel with this class of operations there exist other operations of a spatio-temporal (infralogical) character, and it is these operations that engender the idea of space. The function of the infralogical operations is to produce an object, rather than a collection of objects. Infralogical operations deal not with class inclusion, but with part-whole inclusion for single objects. As Piaget observes,

They substitute the concept of proximity for that of resemblance, difference of order or position ... for difference in general, and the concept of measurement for that of number. Once expressed in propositional form they are indistinguishable from logico-arithmetical operations, of which they constitute merely a particular species, that of continuity as opposed to discontinuity operations. [Piaget and Inhelder 1967, p. 450]

Because they deal with wholes or complete objects, infralogical operations give rise to symbolic images that are clearer and more adequate than those that accompany class or number concepts.

Piaget's statement that actions precede conceptions has a particular application to spatial conceptions. It was noted earlier that spatial perception takes place in the presence of the object, whereas the conceptual image forms in its absence. Perceptual space develops more rapidly than does conceptual space, often resulting in a difference of several years between perceptual and conceptual construction. The assimilation of images and actions together is the means by which progress is made from percept to concept. Furthermore, Piaget points out:

> As regards action itself, we have time and again seen that it plays a far more fundamental role than does the image. Geometrical intuition is essentially active in character. It consists primarily of virtual actions, abridgements or schemata of past, or anticipatory schemata of future actions, and if the action itself is inadequate, intuition breaks down. [Piaget and Inhelder 1967, p. 452]

All of the forms of spatial intuition that Piaget has studied have depended upon actions, ranging from elementary serial relations (arranging objects in two directions) to surrounding (knots) to projective relations (perspective, shadows, plane rotations) and so on, through coordination of groups and diagrammatic layouts: "these have been actions like putting things next to one another (proximity) or in series (order), actions of enclosing, of tightening or loosening, changing viewpoints, cutting, rotating, folding or unfolding, enlarging or reducing, and so on" (pp. 452–53). Piaget believes that spatial concepts are internalized actions and not merely mental images of external objects or events, or of the results of these actions:

> Spatial concepts can only effectively predict these results by becoming active themselves, by operating on physical objects, and not simply by evoking memory images of them. To arrange objects mentally is not merely to imagine a series of things

already set in order, nor even to imagine the action of arranging them. It means arranging the series, just as positively and actively as if the action were physical, but performing the action internally on symbolic objects. [Piaget and Inhelder 1967, p. 454]

He concludes that it is erroneous to conceive of spatial intuition as merely a system of images, because the intuitions involve actions, which the image may symbolize but cannot replace.

The difference between the image stemming from logical operations and the image founded on infralogical operations lies in the function of the image, a difference that will help clarify the basic distinction between these two kinds of operations. Piaget observes that

A spatial field is a single schema embracing all the elements of which it is composed and uniting them in one monolithic bloc, whereas a logical class is a collection of discontinuous elements linked by their resemblance, regardless of spatio-temporal location. [Piaget and Inhelder 1967, p. 456]

The image resulting from spatial operations is always far more complete and more nearly like its referent object or system. By contrast, the image symbolizing the product of a logical operation represents only a part of the whole system, and is at best incomplete.

Further clarification of the distinctions between these two fundamental classes of operations can be achieved through recognition of the fact that logical operations deal with individual objects considered as invariants; they are concerned with linking these objects together or interrelating them, irrespective of their spatio-temporal location. In contrast, infralogical operations deal with the creation of entities from their elements. For example, this might mean fusing the parts of an object into a single whole, or by arranging the parts in some specific order. These infralogical relations link or segregate objects in terms of proximity and distance. Piaget believes that infralogical operations cannot be considered as simply a special class of logical operations, a conclusion that might seem plausible if proximities or separations were not regarded as unique relationships, and if the parts of objects were regarded as whole objects in and of themselves. Such assumptions are not valid, however, because, as Piaget points out:

linking items together on the basis of proximity results in unitary wholes whose ultimate outcome is continuity. . . . On the other hand, items brought together on the basis of similarity result in discontinuous systems, so that sub-logical [infralogical] operations cannot be regarded as equivalent with logical operations. [Piaget and Inhelder 1967, p. 458]

Harvey (1969), drawing upon the work of Carnap (1958), Wilson (1955), and several papers by M. F. Dacey, has developed a somewhat similar analysis of the problem of ordering geographic information and identifying what he calls the "geographical individual." He points out that the geographer is required to use either of two "languages" for identifying and grouping individuals: one a "substance language" which characterizes objects in terms of their inherent properties (logico-arithmetic), the other a "space-time language" (spatio-temporal) which characterizes the things or objects in terms of their locations. Harvey observes:

These languages identify two different kinds of individuals possessing different properties. The notion of similarity or "sameness," for example, relies upon the properties of two individuals being the same in the substance language, but relies upon two individuals occupying the same position in the space-time language. Geographers, in attempting to order information, have never quite sorted out which language they are using, and in regionalization frequently appear to mix the two. [1969, p. 216]

It is clear from Piaget's work that every person does not go completely through all the possible developmental stages he describes, and, in consequence, not every mind can achieve a complete and ultimate development of representational space. In fact, it seems likely that those who attain that conception are in the minority. Blanshard makes a similar observation:

space is simply a relation of systematized outsideness, by itself neither sensible nor imaginable. Of course most minds never come near such a conception, as indeed for all ordinary purposes it is unnecessary that they should. [1948, 1:525]

It is reasonable to assume, then, that there may be much about any map that may go unperceived for lack of appropriate spatial constructs on the part of some percipients. The map contains the potential for extremely sophisticated analysis, both in terms of the geometric systems displayed and in terms of the logical and infralogical operations that may be performed because of it. But such potential is probably not often realized—even by the cartographer who made the map.

Another significant and useful way of viewing spatial knowledge, different from Piaget's presentation, though in no way contradictory, has been developed by Polanyi. Central to Polanyi's argument is the belief that all knowledge is ultimately personal, rooted in and affected by ways of believing and valuing that the knower has internalized. There is no such thing as an objective fact, existing immutably in some objective universe unaffected by the nature of the knower and his assumptions. Polanyi distinguishes between two kinds of knowledge, *tacit* and *explicit,* and builds his presentation with examples that are dominantly spatial and that often invoke the image of the map:

> What is usually described as knowledge, as set out in written words or maps, or mathematical formulae, is only one kind of knowledge; while unformulated knowledge, such as we have of something we are in the act of doing, is another form of knowledge. If we call the first kind explicit knowledge, and the second, tacit knowledge, we may say that *we always know tacitly that we are holding our explicit knowledge to be true.* [1963, p. 12]

Polanyi argues that tacit knowing is in fact the dominant principle of all knowledge. In the area of spatial conceptions, the distinction he makes between these two kinds of knowing is closely related to the distinction Piaget makes between our knowledge of perceptual space (where we act and operate) and representational space (where we *think* about action).

In Polanyi's view, the knower is an active being, not a passive absorber of information. Making sense of experience, comprehension, and "reorganizing our experience so as to gain intellectual control over it" (1959, p. 20)—all these are included in the act of understanding. In dealing with explicit knowledge, we are able to reflect critically on what we know, because the form the knowledge takes is external to ourselves. But in the domain of inarticulate tacit knowledge, what is known cannot be so analyzed (p. 17): "Knowledge acquired and held in this manner may therefore be called a-critical." Polanyi uses the example of a map to illustrate this difference. A man, he begins,

> . . . may be provided with a detailed map of a region through which he is passing. The advantage of a map is obvious, both

for the information which it conveys and for the more important reason that it is much easier to trace an itinerary on a map than to plan it without a map. But there is also a new risk involved in traveling by a map: namely that the map may be mistaken. And this is where critical reflection comes in. The peculiar risk that we take in relying on any explicitly formulated knowledge is matched by a peculiar opportunity offered by explicit knowledge for reflecting on it critically. We can check the information embodied in a map, for example, by reading it at some place that we can directly survey and compare the map with the landmarks in front of us. [p. 15]

We can do this with a map for two reasons:

First, because a map is a thing external to us and not something we are ourselves doing or shaping, and second, because even though it is merely an external object, it can yet speak to us. It tells us something to which we can listen. It does that equally, whether we have drawn the map ourselves or bought it in a shop, but for the moment it is the former case that we are interested in, namely when the map is in fact a statement of our own.... We may listen to it in a critical manner ... any number of times.... Obviously nothing quite like this can take place on the pre-articulate level. I can test the kind of mental map I possess of a familiar region only in action, that is, by actually using it as my guide. If I then lose my way, I can correct my ideas accordingly. There is no other way of improving inarticulate [tacit] knowledge. [p. 16]

Polanyi suggests that the understanding of words and other symbols is a tacit process. Words can convey information and a map can show the topography of a region, but neither the words nor the map can be said to communicate an understanding of themselves:

Though such statements will be made in a form which best induces an understanding of their message, the sender of the message will always have to rely for the comprehension of his message on the intelligence of the person addressed. Only by virtue of this act of comprehension, of this tacit contribution of his own, can the receiving person be said to acquire knowledge when he is presented with a statement. [1959, p. 22]

Here, very concisely stated, is an insight that is missing from much current writing on the general subject of communication, in cartography as well as elsewhere. The sender of any message, the mapmaker included, can only *induce an understanding;* the form in which the information is presented has certain probabilities of mutual meaning associated with it. The map is not a carefully prepared set of objective information, inserted like an electrode into the mind of a viewer. Instead, the viewer, the percipient, must assemble meaning on the basis of the graphic display presented to him, by combining his tacit knowledge and the explicit knowledge of the map before he can truly be said to apprehend meaning from the map.

Polanyi again refers to spatial knowledge as he explains how meaning is acquired from explicit formulations such as type, pictures, maps, and mathematical symbols, and how, when real "understanding" is achieved, it is converted into a different form of personal, tacit knowledge. From clearly specified particulars or parts, the unspecifiable whole may ultimately be derived. Although he takes his example from human anatomy, the parallel with the content of maps is obvious. The medical student learns long lists of bones, muscles, and so on, the elements that constitute the subject matter of systematic anatomy. Except for the task of memorizing them, the names and functions, as they are known, present no real problem in understanding. The major difficulty, however, arises from the fact that the student must grasp mentally the intricate three-dimensional arrangement of bones, arteries, veins, ganglia, tubes, and organs closely packed within the body; but no one diagram or model can give a completely satisfactory representation. As Polanyi points out:

> It is left to the imagination to reconstruct from such experience [as layer-by-layer dissection] the three-dimensional picture of the exposed area as it existed in the unopened body. . . . This kind of topographic knowledge which an experienced surgeon possesses of the regions on which he operates is therefore ineffable [tacit] knowledge. [1964, p. 89]

Polanyi continues that even if the student were presented with a thousand successive thin sections, and if he were to memorize in detail each cross-section,

> He would know a set of data which fully determine the spatial arrangement of the organs in the body; yet he would not know that spatial arrangement itself. Indeed, the cross-sections which

he knows would be incomprehensible and useless to him, until
he could interpret them in the light of this so far unknown
arrangement; while on the other hand, had he achieved this
topographic understanding, he could derive an indefinite
amount of further new and significant information from his
understanding, *just as one reads off [innumerable] itineraries
from a map.* [italics added]

In comprehending the whole, attention must shift from the
particulars to an understanding of their joint meaning. In seeing the
whole, we must see the parts, of course, but the manner in which we
see the parts must change. It is clear that Polanyi distinguishes two
kinds of seeing—one that produces total, focal awareness and one
that produces fragmentary, subsidiary awareness. These two kinds
of apprehension, of ways in which we acquire knowledge, as when
looking at a map, turn out to be at the heart of one of the
fundamental distinctions in cartography. As we shall see in the next
chapter, the percipient's comprehension of the milieu as portrayed
on a map may occur in one way or the other, preferably in
accordance with the objective of the cartographer.

The analysis of the acquisition and character of spatial knowledge
in this chapter may seem inordinately theoretical to the cartographer; but, as we have tried to show, the complex nature of
conceptual space must be taken into account whenever any map is
made. The reader must by now realize that a cartographer's
conceptions of space are not necessarily those of a percipient; if the
cartographer is to induce understanding, he must appreciate the
possible spatial constructs the percipient brings to the map. The
cartographer cannot safely proceed on the belief that maps can be
composed of objective parts of reality as simply ordered by "nature's
own design." This limited discussion of the penetrating analyses of
Piaget and Polanyi in this area should motivate even the most
dogmatic mapper to scrutinize the nature of his own tacit knowledge
about mapping.

6 Structure in Maps and Mapping

> The world is presented in a kaleidoscopic flux of impressions which has to be organized by our minds.
>
> B. L. Whorf

Our review in Chapter 2 of the map as a medium of communication noted that recent methodologic writings in cartography have emphasized that the percipient is an integral functioning component. It was observed, however, that the models of cartography which have been devised are essentially activity-oriented descriptions of the field rather than attempts to discover its basic character or probings of its theoretical foundations. The great majority of research in cartography has been concerned with a variety of significant practical and technical applications in such areas as orthophoto mapping, map transformations (projections), automation, the portrayal of quantitative data, and user reactions. Much less attention has been devoted to its philosophical aspects, and only rarely has research in cartography been much concerned with the primary element in the mapping process, namely the cognitive character of the mapper as both a cartographer and a percipient.

Although cartography is often dubbed "an art and science," it is important to understand that it is also an exercise in engineering (Bartz 1972). This is not to say that there is no intuitive component in cartography (or engineering); "artistic" creativity is recognized as an integral part of the design process in the construction of any functional object (Blumrich 1970). Architecture is a particularly relevant parallel to cartography (Robinson 1952, pp. 13–14). Nevertheless, except for the occasional map that is primarily decorative, a map is constructed fundamentally to accomplish one or more informative purposes; like any utilitarian article, it must be designed with primary attention to its functioning. Recent developments in cartography have been phenomenal. This is especially true of the technical aspects: as new methods and products of cartographic ingenuity are developed and applied, we can look forward to a continuous and exciting transformation of the field. But the real basis for evaluating such things as manual landform representation, or systems of computer hill shading, or methods of generalization, or the orthophoto map, lies not in the reduction of cost, the lessening of the lag time between the beginning and the completion of a map, or in the map's popular appeal, but is to be found in the character of the percepts the map marks actually induce. The worth of all research in cartography, whether the investigation be evaluative or innovative, technical or philosophical, must ultimately be judged on functional, perceptual–cognitive grounds.

For that reason we have attempted, so far in this book, to adduce some of the human cognitive characteristics that lead to an understanding of mapping as one of man's basic forms of knowing and communicating. None are peculiarly cartographic, but we feel that such things as the nature of meaning, the mimetic-arbitrary continuum in symbology, the mechanisms of seeing and visual processing, the part-whole phenomenon, logical and infralogical operations, and topological, projective, and Euclidean referencings are basic to man as a mapper and hence to an understanding of the nature of cartography. Some of the topics we have discussed are of general relevance to the conception of man as a being with intellectual capacities, but some, such as the conception of space, the part-whole comprehension, and the logical-infralogical ways of establishing relations, have unusual significance to mapping.

In this chapter we shall explore the cartographic implications of certain of these cognitive operations, an analysis that leads us ultimately to a hypothesis concerning the logical basis for the generally accepted classification of maps and mapping processes, namely the functional classes of thematic and general (or reference) maps, on the one hand, and the dimensional classes, large- and small-scale, on the other. The arguments and conceptions bridging the logical and functional approaches are sufficiently intricate that they must be examined in some detail, one at a time, then "held in mind" until the relations among them can be examined simultaneously. The three topics to be examined separately and then integrated in such a way that they become cartographically relevant are: (1) levels of spatial articulation of the milieu, (a concept developed by the authors), (2) modes of logical operation as developed by Piaget and his associates, and (3) the nature of scale manipulation as the process which links discrete modes of logical operation and allows the division of maps into logically and functionally discrete categories. To show how the fundamental classes of mapping appear to be related to and a consequence of cognitive operations, we shall begin by considering the basic operations involved in the apprehension of the milieu.

The milieu consists of both tangible and intangible components arrayed in space. To be mapped these components must be observed, and throughout our previous discussions we have generally taken the overall act of apprehension for granted. But the systematic allocation of meaning to things in space is not a simple operation; it involves an essential discriminatory appraisal, as described by Cassirer:

> Every articulation in space presupposes an articulation in judgment; differences in position, size, and distance can only be grasped and assigned because the separate sensory impressions are differently regarded by the judgment, because a different *significance* is imputed to them. [1957, 2:130]

Furthermore, one can focus on spatial attributes or carry out operations leading to spatial articulation at three distinct levels: existence, location, and structure. These three are related in a nested way. The fact of existence can be apprehended without imputing to the object the characteristic of either location or structure, but location must incorporate the attribute of existence, while structure necessarily embraces (but is not limited to) the properties of both existence and location.

In the assignment of meaning at the first level, that of existence alone, we are aware only of the fact of occurrence. The item in question can consist of whatever we consider a "thing"; it can be anything conceived as an object—a road, a city, a state, or even an intangible such as mercury pollution. In establishing the existence of a discrete thing, a primary segregation takes place, our attention focusing on one element in the universe of phenomena comprising the milieu. It must occupy some unique position in space, but that position is of no interest at this level. No spatial association between this object and any other object in the milieu is considered. This conception is, of course, the common non-geographical view utilized in many physical and natural sciences, in that the attribute of the "whereness" of any one object of a class is not considered to be significant. The first level, existence, is clearly not specific to cartography.

The second level, location, is equivalent to the common meaning of that term. Here the object of attention is considered in at least some kind of association or correlation with some other object or portion of the milieu, and that association is essentially spatial; for example, we recognize that city A is near lake B, or country C is in western Europe, or point D occurs at some position within a grid system. The object of attention, at this level of consideration, is not spatially articulated within itself, that is, for the purpose of the level of location the phenomenon is still conceived as a single entity, but it has been endowed with the additional attribute of "whereness." Although one may clearly know that a city comprises various sections and neighborhoods, or a lake has embayments and islands, such heterogeneity is not the subject of attention at this level, and the object is treated as if it were homogeneous and uncomplicated.

Every phenomenon or object exists at a location that can be described relatively, that is, by setting the object in some spatial relation with another object or part of an object. The disposition most often employed at the level of location is either simply topological or is achieved in some very primitive kind of projective space: a mental, nonmetrical transformation of real space that maintains some basic geometric relationships. In the topological conception of space, an object is examined on itself; one employs characteristics, such as connections, enclosure, proximity, and so on, involving no reference to a point of view outside the object. Ordinarily, we tend to describe locations in topological terms; for example, city X is near some other city, town Y is in the bend of river Z, and so on. There need be no reference to projective space or to an all-inclusive spatial framework in these instances: two related phenomena may be considered as if they constitute the total universe of space. At the more sophisticated end of the continuum of the property of geographical location, still at the level of location, we can accomplish the positioning of an object in overall Euclidean terms such as might be generated through the use of latitude and longitude or a less sophisticated rectangular grid system.

The third level, that of structure, is much the most complex of the three classes of spatial articulation. Commonly, the term "structure" has different meanings in various contexts, but on the other hand, its connotation seems to be so well accepted, as we observed in Chapter 1, that many who use it in philosophical discourse treat it as an undefined, a priori, concept. Regardless of the connotation that "structure" may have in other contexts, in cartography we endow it with a specific meaning, albeit a complex one. An important component of our definition of "structure" in cartography is imagery, where the spatial structure of something is comprehended by means of a mental pictorial response. We shall begin our discussion with an illustration.

Suppose that in July we notice drops of water falling on the sidewalk (the first level of spatial articulation), and we conclude that it is raining. Next, we consider the larger location of the rain, say for example, in a town in western Illinois. The meaningfulness of such a locative description would depend on one's knowledge of the immediate milieu: this is, of course, the second level of spatial articulation. If we had an interest in such matters, we could mark on a map the point at which it rains, or we could sum the amount of rain which fell at this point during July and write that figure on the map. Further, we could obtain and plot the average July rainfall at other observing stations in Illinois, or we could extend this record by plotting the appropriate numerical averages for all the observing stations in the entire United States. All of this would still be at the second level of spatial articulation, since a simple assembly of numerals (existences) at places (locations) does not automatically contain the quality of structure. Suppose, however, that we then perform the standard procedures necessary to convert these point-location data into a continuous, conceptual statistical surface portrayed by a layer-tinted isarithmic map, partitioned into classes (Robinson 1961). The average rainfall for July would then be presented in such a way that its variation throughout the United States has been given the attribute of a totality of a related internal and external organization. It is this overall morphological meaningfulness that we call structure.

To the knowledgeable percipient the quality of structure makes possible the operation of the process of geographical inference (inductive generalization: Robinson and Sale 1969, ·p. 58) which follows from an understanding of the symbolic system and the spatial correlation of the phenomenon mapped. Maps can provide this structure for the spatial milieu in a way no other medium can, and it is this attribute of cartography to which Toulmin refers:

> This of course is the marvel of cartography: the fact that, from a limited number of highly precise and well chosen measurements and observations, one can produce a map from which can be read off an unlimited number of geographical facts of almost as great a precision. [1960, pp. 110–11]

If one knows the characteristic spatial structure of some variable, one can infer occurrences at locations without specifically knowing them. In our example, the map of July precipitation needs to employ only selected isohyets, or a map showing hilly terrain by means of contours needs to employ only a relatively few lines, because the precipitation (or elevation) of any point can be inferred from the "meaningful" patterns of the lines. This meaningfulness is possible only because of the nature of earth-space, which is continuous at all points. Knowing just what kind of surface regularity we are dealing with, we can infer specifics from the general structure.

Any portion of a total structure may be isolated and examined as a self-contained unit at the level of location, but when that is done the structure itself is not the subject of focal awareness. There is in the third level of spatial articulation a totality of meaning which goes far beyond the parts of which it is composed. In cartography representational techniques may be chosen so that particular structures are emphasized, or made subordinate. For example, a set of roads may be clearly visible on a point-by-point basis in one presentation, but might have no apparent structure; yet in another representation the systematic organization of the network may become readily apparent because of different line weights, or hue-value contrasts. We emphasize that the elicitation of the conception of structure in the percipient is likely to be more often a function of the cartographic technique than of simply the subject matter and scale.

Another important point needs to be emphasized, namely that at the third level we make an important distinction between the concepts of visual form, on the one hand, and meaningful structure on the other. A portion of reality, or a map of it, might clearly have form, without having what we are calling structure, just as, for example, a pile of machine parts lying in a functionless heap would have visual form, but no structure. Obviously, then, while mere proximity of things may be sufficient in some cases to induce a coherent visual image, proximity alone does not assure that structure will result. It is fundamental to understand that structure, in the sense we are using the term, involves the conception of a *meaningful relationship* among the parts which have been made to appear as a whole. Polanyi employs the term "joint meaning" for a concept similar to our notion of spatial structure when he writes that "when we comprehend a particular set of items as parts of a whole, the focus of our attention is shifted from the hitherto uncomprehended particulars to the understanding of their joint meaning" (1963, p. 29). We stress that there does not seem to be anything in the nature of reality which is structured a priori. Structure is what is attributed by an observer to some arrangement of components which has more meaning than that obtained from simply an aggregation of the parts. It follows then that while a graphic stimulus array may have the potential for being regarded as having structure, the actual conception or realization of that structure must be provided by the percipient.

There appear to be two distinct operational systems underlying our spatial articulation of the milieu, or its surrogate, the map. These have been described in the preceding chapter, where it was explained that they were recognized in studies of the development of the conception of space in the child. Piaget and his associates refer to such spatial articulation as a "logical" operation, and they identify the two ways of establishing relations as "logico-arithmetical" and "spatio-temporal." (We point out again that labeling of the operations producing these relations as "logical" and "infralogical," respectively, is rather unfortunate. Neither operation is related to the concept of "logic," nor is one more "rational" than the other.) The two operations are disparate and lead to two quite different ways of analyzing and synthesizing the perceptually discrete aspects of the milieu. They are distinguished by the different meanings taken on in each of them by the notions of "similarity" and "dissimilarity."

In the logical (logico-arithmetical) approach, objects are judged to be similar or different on the basis of whether they are alike or unlike in their intrinsic characteristics, such as color, shape, size, etc. In establishing infralogical (spatio-temporal) relations, the parallel distinction between being similar or different involves spatial considerations: whether the objects are proximate or separate. For example, Piaget and Inhelder point out:

> Thus two objects may belong to the same logical class, however far apart spatially, if they are similar. And two objects are spatially related so long as they are adjacent, however much they may differ. [1967, p. 431]

It follows, then, that some components of the milieu have the potential of forming a structural entity—the elements or parts can be fused into a single whole, if they are conceived as being proximate in the infralogical mode (with the manipulation of conceptual scale being an important factor, as we shall show). The judgment that the components are spatially related is critical. On the other hand, when the logical mode of operation dominates, the components are not thought of as being spatially related, but instead are linked on the basis of their intrinsic character, with their individual locations being independent of one another.

The operations performed on the milieu in the course of geographical enquiry and cartographic depiction are unique in comparison to the way phenomena are studied by scholars with other objectives. Scholars with non–geographic-cartographic interests tend generally to group the objects of their study on the logical basis of intrinsic resemblances or differences among members. In contrast, the geographic-cartographic approach requires that the objects in the milieu be classified both on that basis and simultaneously on the infralogical basis of their constituting a spatial totality wherein the concepts of spatial proximity or separation are potentially just as meaningful as those of intrinsic likeness or unlikeness. Thus the geographical milieu can be apprehended by the intellect *at one and the same time* on the basis of both kinds of logical operations that Piaget described. In fact, the normally functioning adult will probably always be performing both logical and infralogical operations on the milieu, with more emphasis on one or the other depending on circumstances, interests, and talents. It seems inevitable that the basic classes of mapping should correspondingly reflect the differential dominance of one or the other of those fundamentally distinct modes of logical operation. In order to demonstrate that this, in fact, does seem to be the case we shall first examine briefly the ways in which maps are classified.

Classification is a very complex operation with many purposes. One of these aims is to describe the "natural system," or, as Sokahl puts it "to describe objects in such a way that their true relationships are displayed" (1974, p. 1116). To do this to the satisfaction of all requires that characteristics deemed to be distinctive actually turn out to be so. This is very difficult in many cases, as Sokahl observes, and when the distinguishing properties are not well chosen, it often leads to classes which are not mutually exclusive. Fortunately, as we shall see, the subject of mapping seems not to involve difficulty in this respect when the properties employed are the cognitive objectives of the mapper and the percipient. Because maps are basically utilitarian—they are communicative devices—we might expect, therefore, that an organized inventory of their uses and/or the subjects mapped would lead toward such a "natural system" of classification, and, in fact, this has been the usual path to what categorizing has been done.

Maps are used for a multitude of purposes. As a surrogate for space a map can serve as a medium for many of the operations involving space which one may wish to pursue. These encompass such activities as the recognition of shape and form, differentiation, association, mensuration, prediction, and many others. In addition, of course, the reduction of real space to the manageable proportions of a map makes it possible to extend these operations over greater areas and allows additional deductive activities, such as navigation. The selected characteristics of the milieu that can be mapped are equally varied, ranging from concrete observable phenomena, such as vegetation or elevation, to abstract conceptions, such as religion or population potential.

One would expect that the extraordinary versatility of maps and the enormous range of mappable subject matter and scales would have led early to a logical partitioning of the field on theoretical grounds, but in fact this has occurred only recently. Throughout most of the long history of cartography the lack of a rational classification of maps caused no difficulty, and the relationship among kinds of maps and mapping was not even recognized as an interesting subject of study until not long ago. As a matter of fact, from the earliest times until the nineteenth century, most maps, regardless of scale, were essentially alike from the point of view of their basic function as portrayers of the milieu. They simply recorded and displayed the locations of selected, individual components of the milieu. The chosen categories of information might be quite varied, ranging from roads to boundaries, from canals to coastlines, and from cities to islands, but their essential function was clearly to provide information on objects of the milieu at the second level of spatial articulation, location. They were made primarily to show simply what was where. Topical subclasses of general maps can be recognized in which a limited category of information is emphasized, such as road maps or navigational charts. There seems never to have been any consensus regarding a term to encompass this large group of maps, but in recent times they have been referred to as "reference" or "general" maps. We prefer the latter term because it lacks any specific connotation.

In the late seventeenth century, a very different kind of map began to appear. Among the earliest of such maps were those of winds and magnetic declination by Edmond Halley (Thrower 1969). In the first half of the nineteenth century maps of many other phenomena, such as vegetation, temperature, population, trade, and geology, were made, reflecting the broadening interest in natural, social, and economic phenomena. These maps were not at all like general maps. Instead, each of these maps dealt primarily with a single category of information with the focus on variation from place to place rather than on individual locations. The primary concern was with the third—structural—level of spatial articulation. Such maps were called special-purpose maps, or geographic maps, and they are often simply named from the subject mapped, such as "population," "temperature," etc. This class did not gain the advantage of universal recognition by one name until Creutzberg (1953) coined the term "thematic." Since then the name "thematic" has become generally accepted and is a part of the vocabulary of all cartographers. It has generally come to be associated loosely with maps which delineate individual categories of phenomena.

The totality of maps may also be divided on a dimensional basis according to their scales. As was the case with the general–thematic dichotomy, no real distinction among maps on the basis of scale seems to have been recognized until relatively late in the history of cartography. To be sure, Claudius Ptolemy in the second century A.D. did appreciate the desirability of preparing larger-scale maps of individual sections of the known world, but even those maps would have been classed as small-scale today. During the sixteenth century an interest grew in the detailed mapping of estates, counties, and other particular areas, but it was not until the following century, and especially during the second half of the eighteenth, that the necessary survey techniques were sufficiently developed to allow really large-scale mapping of considerable areas, with the 1:86,400 *Carte Géometrique de la France* (*Carte de Cassini*) setting the style. Since that time the large-scale "topographic" map, for which the locational details are obtained by field or photogrammetric methods, has been contrasted with the small-scale map prepared from compiled rather than surveyed data. The manifold differences between large- and small-scale cartography have been universally recognized as dividing the field into two separate branches. The place on the continuum where the transition from large- to small-scale occurs is at present variably and arbitrarily identified. Nevertheless, the large-scale/small-scale division separates the world of maps, mapping, and cartographers into dimensional categories every bit as distinct as the general/thematic functional categories.

The basic classes of maps and the professional divisions among cartographers have grown up over many years in a rather haphazard fashion. That there are strong forces operating to create the pattern that has evolved seems only reasonable, for it is hard to imagine that such a consensus among so many individuals with such diverse backgrounds could develop by chance. We hypothesize that the foundation for these divisions may well be based on the logical and infralogical operational systems with which we seem to articulate the milieu. The different combinations of these operations logically lead to large- or small-scale categories of mapping, on the one hand, and thematic or general mapping on the other. The basic difference between the logical and infralogical intellectual operations which seems to underlie general and thematic mapping serves also to emphasize the importance of the cognitive contrast between the locational and structural articulations of the milieu which is the fundamental difference between the two kinds of mapping.

To show the possible combinations among the kinds of operations and how they may lead to the fundamental classes of maps we can cross-classify the types of judgments involved to form the matrix shown in Fig. 6.1. The matrix presents four pairs of combinations, two in the rows and two in the columns. Each pair of combinations in a row or a column leads, as shown by the arrows, to a major class of mapping. In interpreting the matrix two important facts should be kept in mind. One is that, as previously observed, the logical (alike-unlike) and infralogical (proximate-separate) operations always occur in combination, with one or the other being dominant depending upon the objective of the cartographer. The second is that while the matrix implies the result of cross-classification to be four discrete classes, it must be emphasized that the functional classes of thematic and general mapping, on the one hand, and the dimensional classes of large- and small-scale mapping on the other, should be viewed as two continua. Pure general mapping shades into thematic mapping and obvious large-scale shades into small-scale. A closer look at the combinations of the matrix will make clear the kinds of operational interactions that produce the classes.

The combinations A1 and B1 in the upper row of Fig. 6.1 lead to the functional class of general mapping. A geographical area of interest of the milieu—one in which all referents can be considered as proximate or "near"—is partitioned off, so to speak, for Class A1, and the cartographer then locates and maps a selection of its unlike characteristics, such as streams, roads, buildings, elevations, survey lines, vegetation, etc. In so doing his concern is directed toward the second level of spatial articulation, location, as previously described. The percipient turns to such a map to answer the questions "What is at point X?" and "Where is phenomenon Y?" Class B1 is functionally like class A1 in that location is the focus of interest, but class B1 consists of maps of separate areas rather than of a single, proximate area.

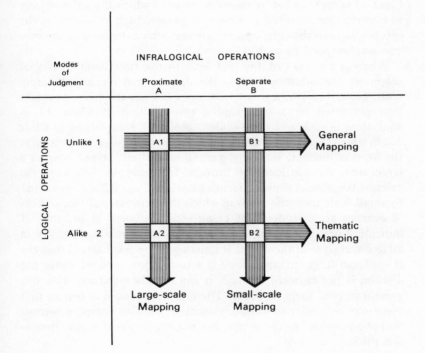

Fig. 6.1. A cross classification of logical and infralogical modes of operation and the classes of mapping to which the several combinations lead.

Classes A2 and B2 of Fig. 6.1 lead to the functional class of thematic mapping. In category A2 a limited, that is proximate, geographical area of the milieu is brought into focus, and in this case the variations of a single, alike characteristic, or some single defined relationship among two or more characteristics is mapped. As pointed out above, in thematic mapping the cartographer is primarily concerned with the third level of spatial articulation, structure, and consequently, attempts to induce the feeling for structure in the percipient by the graphic technique (Robinson 1961; Sherman 1961, p. 17). Examples of class A2 would be a map of an orange growing area in California portraying simply its shape, or a map of the population density of an area showing the variations in the relation between numbers of people and the areas they inhabit. Class B2 is represented by thematic maps in which the alike objects of concern are considered as being separate, such as would be the case with a map showing separate areas in which the same phenomenon was mapped in each.

Whereas the rows of Fig. 6.1 lead to the functional classes of mapping, the columns lead to the dimensional classes. A large-scale, general map of a small area, say a few square miles, as might be represented by a topographic map, falling in Class A1 is equivalent in scale to a large-scale, "geologic" map falling in Class A2, in which the detailed distribution of bedrock types in the area is the focus of interest. Similarly, a small-scale, "atlas-type" map of a large area, the continent of Europe, for example, will have the primary function of showing locations, while Class B2 is represented by small-scale thematic maps in which the structures of like objects of concern are considered as being separate, such as in maps of individual orange-growing areas or maps of population density in different regions of the world. It must again be emphasized that the range from large- to small-scale is a continuum, and wherever the division is put between the two, it can only be arbitrary with our present state of understanding. There is some reason to believe that there may be some non-arbitrary division based on complex perceptual phenomena, but the matter has not had any real study (Robinson 1965).

The rationale underlying present practice in the production of general mapping (A1, B1) is very confused and complex. This is especially true in large-scale mapping, since the phenomena mapped are of great variety, often not carefully classified, and the visual hierarchies of their portrayal are often illogical. Many of these problems are treated by Keates (1972), who convincingly argues two hypotheses regarding topographic (general) maps:

> First, that for any feature, only a selection of the total information which describes it is shown by the map symbol: second, that the function of the symbol is mainly to classify or categorize; that is, those features which have certain character-

> istics in common are grouped together, even though they all
> have individual differences, and even though they all have
> different locations [p. 169]

In small-scale general mapping the common practice of displaying
elevational data or the configuration of the landform as a "back-
ground" is followed probably more as a habit than as a consequence
of functional planning. In many parts of the world the socio-
economic aspects of the environment may well today be "more
important" than the physical.

In spite of the fact that the theoretical aspects of general mapping
are as yet not well understood (Robinson 1971) these maps are
readily accepted because they are enormously useful and very
common. On the other hand, thematic mapping is basically straight-
forward; it is simply an attempt to deal with the concept of structure
in the milieu. But because it involves a more complex level of spatial
articulation it is a more sophisticated intellectual task for the
cartographer and the percipient, although emphatically not necessarily more difficult than general mapping. One is therefore not
surprised that thematic mapping is a relatively recent development
in the long history of mapping.

The manipulation of scale in order to achieve structure is of
considerable importance in cartography. In ordinary experience
objects are either considered to be discrete, and therefore amenable
to grouping in logical classes, *or* linked in infralogical terms by
spatial proximity or nearness, and there is ordinarily no link between
the two systems. Mapping is unique, however, in that by the
manipulation of "scale," objects can be transformed from a state of
"separateness" to one of "proximity," allowing the creation of *an*
object from what may also be apprehended as a collection of discrete
objects. This manipulation of scale allows one to shift freely from the
domain of logical operations to that of infralogical operations.
Discrete locations can, through the transformation of scale change,
become components of an integrated structure subject to spatial
rather than, or in addition to, class analysis. Structure, as a level of
spatial articulation, can be achieved when aspects of the earth-object
that are "apart" in normal experience and perception are placed
into immediate proximity, and this is most commonly done through
the reduction of map scale. In the cartographic literature scale is
treated, often implicitly, as one of the most fundamental concepts in
cartography, and heretofore it has been hard to account for its over-

whelming significance. However, with the recognition that the concept of structure and the idea of closeness is critical to conceptualizing the milieu, it is apparent that the importance of scale is well founded.

Scale involves complex concepts and implications with which it is difficult to deal. In its most basic sense the term "scale" refers to the simple, numerically stated relation between a given magnitude of a map, and the real magnitude of the milieu which it represents, usually involving real distance or area in Euclidean terms; but the "unreal" complex scale relationships employed in cartograms may also be involved. "Scale" also refers to the level or depth with which one contemplates or analyzes something, as for example whether one "looks closely" at something or contemplates it "from a distance." The large scale, the close look in cartography, tends to inhibit the focus on structure, perhaps because every variation is a figure, while the distant view, the small-scale in cartography, tends to diminish the separateness of the differences and therefore promotes the appreciation of structure.

It is well to point out that the concepts of "close" and "distant" tend to be relative. They are always a function of the scale of the focus or analysis, where that which is far in sensory experience may be very different from that which is near, for example, in mentally contemplating geologic characteristics at the world scale. Cartography is fundamentally involved in this close–distant conception, for by mapping we are able to change our sensory input from that which is separate in everyday experience to that which is proximate as we look at a particular map. One of the most elegant things about thematic mapping, in fact, is that it makes it possible for us to achieve a total view of phenomena when that view is not possible in any other way. There may well be a preferred scale for each phenomenon being mapped thematically, as asserted by Miller and Voskuil (1964), who argue that we search for this "correct" scale in any thematic mapping activity.

The basic topological concept of "closeness-at-a-scale" seems to be a functional element in cartography and much of geography. In a sense, even such logical processes as differentiation and scaling involve this same idea. Ordering systems higher than nominal (i.e., ordinal, interval, and ratio) are commonly conceived as though the groupings were arrayed in space along a linear continuum. Because the range of values included and the division of the continuum into sub-spaces is then related to a sense of what constitutes a meaningful proximity in a conceptual scale sense, the enormous significance of the concept of scale becomes apparent. The reason for the common use of mapping as a metaphor for knowing or communicating, as noted in Chapter 1, has finally become clear: the concept of spatial relatedness which is of concern in mapping and which indeed is the reason for the very existence of cartography, is a quality without which it is difficult or impossible for the human mind to apprehend anything.

References

Adams, R. P. 1974. On the necessity of literature. *AAUP Bulletin* 60:24–26.

Adler, B. F. 1911. *Maps of primitive peoples*. St. Petersburg, 1910. Translated and abridged by H. de Hutorowicz, *Bulletin of the American Geographical Society* 43:669–679.

Arnberger, E. 1974. Problems of an international standardization of a means of communication through cartographic symbols. *International Yearbook of Cartography* 14:19–35.

Arnheim, R. 1964. *Art and visual perception*. Berkeley: University of California Press.

Bagrow, L. 1948. Eskimo maps. *Imago Mundi* 5:92–94.

Balasubramanyan, V. 1971. Application of information theory to maps. *International Yearbook of Cartography* 11:177–181.

Bar-Hillel, Y. 1964. *Language and information*, Reading, Mass.: Addison-Wesley.

Bartz, B. S. 1967. What about Illinois? or, Children and a reference map. Unpublished study done for Field Enterprises Educational Corporation.

———. 1969a. Type variation and the problem of cartographic type legibility. *Journal of Typographic Research* 3:127–144.

———. 1969b. Search: An approach to cartographic type legibility measurement. *Journal of Typographic Research* 3:387–398.

———. 1970. Experimental use of the search task in an analysis of type legibility in cartography. *Journal of Typographic Research* 4:147–167. Reprinted in *Cartographic Journal* 7:103–112.

———. 1972. The nature of research in education. *Journal of Geography* 71:215–232.

Beller, H. K. 1968. Stages of processing in visual search. Ph.D. diss., Brandeis University.

———. 1972. Problems of visual search. *International Yearbook of Cartography* 12:137–144.

Bertin, J. 1968. Cartography in the computer age. Paper presented at Technical Symposium S 40, ICA–IGU, New Delhi.

———. 1970. La graphique. *Communications* 15:169–184.

———. 1973. *Semiologie graphique*. 2d ed. Paris: Gauthier-Villars.

Blanshard, B. 1948. *The nature of thought*. 2 vols. London: George Allen and Unwin.

Blumenstock, D. I. 1953. The reliability factor in the drawing of isarithms. *Annals of the Association of American Geographers* 43:289–304.

Blumrich, J. F. 1970. Design. *Science* 168:1551–1554.

Board, C. 1967. Maps as models. In *Models in geography*, ed. R. J. Chorley and P. Haggett, pp. 671–725. London: Methuen.

———. 1973. Cartographic communication and standardization. *International Yearbook of Cartography* 13:229–236.

Bronowski, J. 1965. *Science and human values*. New York: Harper and Row.

Bunge, W. L. 1966. *Theoretical geography*. Lund Studies in Geography, series C, no. 1, Lund: C. W. K. Gleerup.

Carnap, R. 1958. *Introduction to symbolic logic and its applications*. Translated by W. H. Meyer and J. Wilkinson. New York: Dover Publications.

Cassirer, E. 1955. *The philosophy of symbolic forms*. Vol. 2. *Mythical thought*. New Haven: Yale University Press.

———. 1957. *The philosophy of symbolic forms*. Vol. 3. *The phenomenology of knowledge*. New Haven: Yale University Press.

Castner, H. W., and McGrath, G., eds. 1971. Map design and the map user. *Cartographica*, monograph no. 2.

Castner, H. W., and Robinson, A. H. 1969. *Dot area symbols in cartography: The influence of pattern on their perception*. Monograph no. CA-4. Washington, D.C.: American Congress on Surveying and Mapping.

Chase, W. G., ed. 1973. *Visual information processing*. New York: Academic Press.

Chorley, R. J., and Haggett, P. 1967. *Models in geography*. London: Methuen.

Clarke, J. I. 1959. Statistical map reading. *Geography* 44:96–104.

Cohen, S. B., ed. 1973. *Oxford world atlas*. New York: Oxford University Press, pp. vi, 14–29.

Coombs, C. H. 1964. *A theory of data*. New York: John Wiley.

Cornwell, B., and Robinson, A. H. 1966. Possibilities for computer-animated films in cartography. *Cartographic Journal* 3:79–82.

Crawford, P. V. 1971. Perception of grey-tone symbols. *Annals of the Association of American Geographers* 61:721–735.

———. 1973. The perception of graduated squares as cartographic symbols. *Cartographic Journal* 10:85–94.

Creutzberg, N. 1953. Zum Problem der thematischen Karten in Atlaswerken. *Kartographische Nachrichten* 3:11–12.

Cuff, D. J. 1972. The magnitude message: A study of the effectiveness of color sequences on quantitative maps. Ph.D. diss., Pennsylvania State University.

———. 1973. Colour on temperature maps. *Cartographic Journal* 10:17–21.

Davis, W. M. 1924. The progress of geography in the United States. *Annals of the Association of American Geographers* 14:159–215.

Dent, B. D. 1971. Perceptual organization and thematic map communications: Some principles for effective map design with special emphasis on the figure ground relationship. Ph.D. diss., Clark University.

———. 1972. Visual organization and thematic map communication. *Annals of the Association of American Geographers* 62:79–93.

———. 1973. Simplifying thematic maps through effective design: Some postulates for the measure of success. *Proceedings of the American Congress on Surveying and Mapping Fall Convention,* pp. 243–251.

Dornbach, J. E. 1967. An analysis of the map as an information display system. Ph.D. diss., Clark University.

———. 1972. The mental map. *Proceedings of the 32d Annual Meeting, American Congress on Surveying and Mapping,* pp. 65–69.

Downs, R. M., and Stea, D. 1973a. *Image and environment.* Chicago: Aldine.

———. 1973b. Cognitive maps and spatial behaviour: Processes and products. In *Image and Environment,* ed. R. M. Downs and D. Stea, pp. 8–26. Chicago: Aldine.

Ekman, G., and Junge, K. 1961. Psychophysical relations in visual perception of length, area, and volume. *Scandinavian Journal of Psychology* 2:1–10.

Ekman, G.; Lindman, R.; and William-Olsson, W. 1961. A psychophysical study of cartographic symbols. *Perceptual and Motor Skills* 13:355–368.

Exton, W. 1951. Human communication: Non-verbal and supra-verbal. *General Semantics Bulletin* 6-7:16-24.

Flannery, J. J. 1956. The graduated circle: A description, analysis and evaluation of a quantitative map symbol. Ph.D. diss., University of Wisconsin.

————. 1971. The relative effectiveness of some common graduated point symbols in the presentation of quantitative data. *Canadian Cartographer* 8:96-109.

Freitag, U. 1971. Semiotik und Kartographie. *Kartographische Nachrichten* 21:171-182.

Frenzel, K. 1965. Zur Frage des optischen Gewichts von Signaturen für thematische Karten. *Erdkunde* 19:66-70.

Furth, H. G. 1969. *Piaget and knowledge*. Englewood Cliffs, N.J.: Prentice-Hall.

Gokhman, V. M.; Meckler, M. M.; and Polezhayev, A. P. 1970. Special and general informative capacity of topical maps. Unpublished paper prepared for the 5th International Cartographic Conference of the ICA.

Gould, P., and White, R. 1974. *Mental maps*. Baltimore: Penguin Books.

Green, R. T., and Courtis, M. C. 1966. Information theory and figure perception: The metaphor that failed. *Acta Psychologica* (Amsterdam) 25:12-36.

Hake, G. 1970. Der Informationsgehalt der Karte—Merkmal und Masze. In *Grundsatzfragen der Kartographie*, pp. 119-131. Vienna: Austrian Geographical Society.

Hall, E. T. 1959. *The silent language*. Greenwich, Conn.: Fawcett Publications.

Hart, R. A., and Moore, G. T. 1973. The development of spatial cognition: A review. In *Image and environment*, ed. R. M. Downs and D. Stea, chap. 14. Chicago: Aldine.

Hartley, R. V. L. 1928. Transmission of information. *Bell System Technical Journal* 7:535-563.

Harvey, D. 1969. *Explanation in geography*. London: Edward Arnold; New York: St. Martin's Press, 1970.

Hayakawa, S. I., ed. 1962. *The use and misuse of language*. Greenwich, Conn.: Fawcett Publications.

Head, G. 1972. Land-water differentiation in black and white cartography. *Canadian Cartographer* 9:25-38.

Heath, W. R. 1967. Cartographic perimeters. *International Yearbook of Cartography* 7:112-120.

Hutorowicz, H. de. 1911. Maps of primitive peoples. *Bulletin of the*

American Geographical Society 42:669–679.

Imhof, E. 1963. Tasks and methods of theoretical cartography. *International Yearbook of Cartography* 3:13–25.

――――. 1965. *Kartographische Geländedarstellung.* Berlin: Walter de Gruyter.

Ivins, W. M., Jr. 1953. *Prints and visual communication.* Cambridge: MIT Press.

Jenks, G. F. 1970. Conceptual and perceptual error in thematic mapping. *Technical Papers,* 30th Annual Meeting of the American Congress on Surveying and Mapping, pp. 174–188.

――――. 1973. Visual integration in thematic mapping: Fact or fiction? *International Yearbook of Cartography* 13:27–35.

Jenks, G. F., and Knos, D. S. 1961. The use of shading patterns in graded series. *Annals of the Association of American Geographers* 51:316–334.

Johnson, F. C., and Klare, G. R. 1961. General models of communication research: A survey of the development of a decade. *Journal of Communication* 2:13–26, 45.

Kádár, I.; Ágfalvi, M.; Lakos, L.; and Karsay, F. 1973. A practical method for estimation of map information content. Unpublished paper presented at meeting of Commission III, ICA, Budapest.

Kates, R. W. 1970. Human perception of the environment. *International Social Science Journal* 22:648–660.

Keates, J. S. 1962. The perception of colour in cartography. *Proceedings of the Cartographic Symposium, Edinburgh,* pp. 19–28.

――――. 1972. Symbols and meaning in topographic maps. *International Yearbook of Cartography* 12:168–181.

Koeman, C. 1971. The principle of communication in cartography. *International Yearbook of Cartography* 11:169–176.

Koláčný, A. 1968. *Cartographic information—A fundamental notion and term in modern cartography.* Prague: Czechoslovak Committee on Cartography (in English).

――――. 1969. Cartographic information—A fundamental term in modern cartography. *Cartographic Journal* 6:47–49.

――――. 1970. Kartographische Information—Ein Grundbegriff und Grundterminus der modernen Kartographie. *International Yearbook of Cartography* 10:186–193.

Korzybski, A. 1941. *Science and sanity.* Lancaster, Pa.: International Non-Aristotelian Library Publishing Company.

Kuhn, T. S. 1962. *The structure of scientific revolutions.* Chicago: University of Chicago Press.

Langer, S. K. 1951. *Philosophy in a new key.* New York: New American Library.

Le Gear, C. E. 1944. Map making by primitive peoples. *Special Libraries* 35:79-83.

Lowenthal, D. 1961. Geography, experience, and imagination: Towards a geographical epistemology. *Annals of the Association of American Geographers* 51:241-260.

Lundberg, U. 1973. Emotional and geographical phenomena in psychophysical research. In *Image and environment,* ed. R. M. Downs and D. Stea, pp. 322-337. Chicago: Aldine.

Lynch, K. 1960. *The image of the city.* Cambridge, Mass.: MIT Press.

McCleary, G. F. 1970. Beyond simple psychophysics: Approaches to the understanding of map perception. *Papers from the 30th Annual Meeting, American Congress on Surveying and Mapping,* pp. 189-209.

Makowski, A. 1967. Aesthetic and utilitarian aspects of colour in cartography. *International Yearbook of Cartography* 7:62-87.

Meihoefer, H.-J. 1973. The visual perception of the circle in thematic maps: Experimental results. *Canadian Cartographer* 10:63-84.

Merriam, M. 1971. Eye noise and map design. *Cartographica,* monograph no. 2, pp. 22-28.

Meynen, E., ed. 1973. *Multilingual dictionary of technical terms in cartography* (ICA Commission II). Wiesbaden: Franz Steiner Verlag GMBH.

Mill, J. S. 1867. *Inaugural address; delivered to the University of St. Andrews, Feb. 1st, 1867.* London: Longmans, Green, Reader and Dryer. P. 33.

Miller, O. M., and Voskuil, R. J. 1964. Thematic map generalization. *Geographical Review* 54:13-19.

Moles, A. A. 1964. Théorie de l'information et message cartographique. *Sciences et enseignement des sciences* 5:11-16.

Molineux, A. 1974. Communication theory and its role in cartography. Unpublished paper presented at ACSM Annual Meeting, St. Louis, March 1974.

Morrison, A. 1971. Experimental maps of road travel speed. *Cartographic Journal* 8:115-132.

Morrison, J. L. 1974. Changing philosophical-technical aspects of thematic cartography. *American Cartographer* 1:5-14.

Muehrcke, P. C. 1969. Visual pattern analysis: A look at maps. Ph.D. diss., University of Michigan.

————. 1970. Trends in cartography. In *Focus on geography, key concepts and teaching strategies*, ed. P. Bacon, pp. 197–225. Washington, D.C.: National Council for the Social Studies.

————. 1972. *Research in thematic cartography*. Resource Paper no. 19, Commission on College Geography, Washington, D.C.: Association of American Geographers.

————. 1973. Some notes on pattern complexity in map design. Unpublished paper prepared for panel discussion "Map Design for the User," ACSM annual meeting, March 1973.

Neisser, U. 1967. *Cognitive psychology*. New York: Appleton-Century-Crofts.

Pearson, K. 1970. The relative visual importance of selected line symbols. Master's thesis, University of Wisconsin.

Petchenik, B. B. 1974. A verbal approach to characterizing the look of maps. *American Cartographer* 1:63–71.

Piaget, J., and Inhelder, B. 1967. *The child's conception of space*. New York: W. W. Norton.

Piaget, J.; Inhelder, B.; and Szeminska, A. 1960. *The child's conception of geometry*. New York: Basic Books.

Pierce, J. R. 1961. *Symbols, signals and noise: The nature of communication*. New York: Harper and Row. Harper Torchbooks, The Science Library.

Pietkiewicz, S. 1965. The evolution of the map definition during the last hundred years. *Actes du XIe Congrès IGU* 4:272–275.

Polanyi, M. 1946. *Science, faith and society*. Chicago: University of Chicago Press.

————. 1963. *The study of man*. Chicago: University of Chicago Press. First Phoenix Edition.

————. 1964. *Personal Knowledge*. New York: Harper and Row.

Post, J. B. 1973. *An atlas of fantasy*. Baltimore: Mirage Press.

Pribram, K. 1969. The neurophysiology of remembering. *Scientific American* 220:73–86.

Rapoport, A. 1952. What is semantics? *American Scientist* 40: 123–135.

Ratajski, L. 1970. Kartologia [Cartology]. *Polish Cartographical Review* 2:97–110.

————. 1971. The methodical basis of the standardization of signs on economic maps. *International Yearbook of Cartography* 11: 137–159.

————. 1972. Cartology. *Geographia Polonica* 21:63–78.

————. 1973. The research structure of theoretical cartography.

International Yearbook of Cartography 13:217-228.

―――. 1974. Commission V of ICA: The tasks it faces. *International Yearbook of Cartography* 14:140-144.

Roberts, J. A. 1962. The topographic map in a world of computers. *Professional Geographer* 14:12-13.

Robinson, A. H. 1952. *The look of maps*. Madison: University of Wisconsin Press.

―――. 1961. The cartographic representation of the statistical surface. *International Yearbook of Cartography* 1:53-63.

―――. 1965a. *Designing maps for scale*. Unpublished report to Field Enterprises Educational Corporation.

―――. 1965b. The future of the international map. *Cartographic Journal* 2:23-26.

―――. 1967. Psychological aspects of color in cartography. *International Yearbook of Cartography* 7:50-59.

―――. 1970. Scaling non-numerical map symbols. *Papers from the 30th Annual Meeting, American Congress on Surveying and Mapping*, pp. 210-216.

―――., moderator. 1971. Discussion: An interchange of ideas and reactions. In *Map design and the map user. Cartographica*, monograph no. 2, pp. 46-53.

―――. 1972. Cartography to come. *Revue de Géographie de Montreal* 26:5-6.

―――. 1973. An international standard symbolism for thematic maps: Approaches and problems. *International Yearbook of Cartography* 13:19-26.

―――. 1976. The image and the map. In *Proceedings, 22d International Geographical Congress 1972*, ed. J. K. Fraser. Toronto: University of Toronto Press, forthcoming.

Robinson, A. H., and Sale, R. D. 1969. *Elements of cartography*. 3d ed. New York: John Wiley.

Runkel, P. J. 1956. Cognitive similarity in facilitating communication. *Sociometry* 19:178-191.

Sanders. R. A., and Porter, P. W. 1974. Shape in revealed mental maps. *Annals of the Association of American Geographers* 64: 258-267.

Salichtchev, K. A. 1967. Le développement de la cartographie thématique et l'Association Cartographique Internationale. *International Yearbook of Cartography* 7:121-128.

―――. 1970. The subject and method of cartography: Contemporary views. Trans. J. R. Gibson. *Canadian Cartographer* 7:77-87.

————. 1973a. Some reflections on the subject and method of cartography after the Sixth International Cartographic Conference. *Canadian Cartographer* 10:106–111.

————. 1973b. Some features of the modern cartography development and their theoretical meaning. *Moskovskiy Universitet, Vestnik, Seriya V Geografia* 2:3–11.

Salichtchev, K. A., and Berliant, A. M. 1973. Méthodes d'utilisation des cartes dans les recherches scientifique. *International Yearbook of Cartography* 13:156–183.

Sauer, C. 1956. The education of a geographer. *Annals of the Association of American Geographers* 46:287–299.

Shannon, C. E., and Weaver, W. 1949. *The mathematical theory of communication.* Urbana: University of Illinois Press.

Sherman, J. C. 1961. New horizons in cartography: Functions, automation, and presentation. *International Yearbook of Cartography* 1:13–19.

————. 1964. Terrain representation and map function. *International Yearbook of Cartography* 4:20–24.

Singh, J. 1966. *Great ideas in information theory, language and cybernetics.* New York: Dovet Publications.

Slobin, D. I. 1971. *Psycholinguistics.* Glenview, Ill.: Scott, Foresman.

Sokahl, R. R. 1974. Classification: Purposes, principles, progress, prospects. *Science* 185:1115–1123.

Stevens, S. S. 1957. On the psychophysical law. *Psychological Review* 64:153–181.

Sukhov, V. I. 1970. Application of information theory in generalization of map contents. *International Yearbook of Cartography* 10:41–47.

Tey, Josephine. 1927. *The man in the queue.* London: Peter Davies. P. 138.

Thrower, N. J. 1969. Edmond Halley as a thematic geo-cartographer. *Annals of the Association of American Geographers* 59:652–676.

Tolman, E. C. 1948. Cognitive maps in rats and men. *Psychological Review* 55:189–208.

————. 1951. Cognitive maps in rats and men. In *Collected Papers in Psychology,* pp. 241–264. Berkeley: University of California Press.

Toulmin, S. 1960. *The philosophy of science: An introduction.* New York: Harper and Row, Harper Torchbooks.

Trowbridge, C. C. 1913. On fundamental methods of orientation and "imaginary" maps. *Science* 38:888-897.

Updike, J. 1960. *Rabbit, Run.* New York: Fawcett World Library.

Wehling, L., and Charters, W., Jr. 1969. Dimensions of teacher beliefs about the teaching process. *American Educational Research Journal* 6:7-30.

Wendt, P. R. 1962. The language of pictures. In *The use and misuse of language,* ed. S. I. Hayakawa, pp. 175-183. Greenwich, Conn.: Fawcett Publications.

Whorf, B. L. 1956. *Language, thought and reality.* New York: John Wiley. P. 213.

Wiener, N. 1948. *Cybernetics.* New York: John Wiley.

Williams, R. L. 1956. *Statistical symbols for maps: Their design and relative values.* New Haven: Map Laboratory, Yale University.

Wilson, N. L. 1955. Space, time, and individuals. *Journal of Philosophy* 52:589-598.

Wood, M. 1968. Visual perception and map design. *Cartographic Journal* 5:54-64.

————. 1972. Human factors in cartographic communication. *Cartographic Journal* 9:123-132.

Woodward, D. 1974. The study of the history of cartography: A suggested framework. *American Cartographer* 1:101-115.

Wright, J. K. 1942. Map makers are human: Comments on the subjective in mapping. *Geographical Review* 32:527-544.

Wright, R. D. 1967. Selection of line weights for solid qualitative line symbols in series on maps. Ph.D. diss., University of Kansas.

Yoeli, P., and Loon, J. 1972. Map symbols and lettering: A two part investigation. European Research Office, United States Army, London (NTIS no. AD741834).

Zelinsky, W. 1973. The first and last frontier of communication: The map as mystery. *Bulletin of the Geography and Map Division, Special Libraries Association,* no. 94 (December), pp. 2-8.

Index

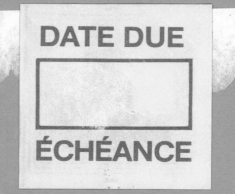